For A...

VEILED THREAT

THE HIDDEN POWER OF THE
WOMEN OF AFGHANISTAN

Best Wishes —

Sally Armstrong

May 29, 2006

SALLY ARMSTRONG

PENGUIN
CANADA

PENGUIN CANADA

Penguin Group (Canada), a division of Pearson Penguin Canada Inc.,
10 Alcorn Avenue, Toronto, Ontario M4V 3B2

Penguin Group (U.K.), 80 Strand, London WC2R 0RL, England
Penguin Group (U.S.), 375 Hudson Street, New York, New York 10014, U.S.A.
Penguin Group (Australia) Inc., 250 Camberwell Road, Camberwell, Victoria 3124, Australia
Penguin Group (Ireland), 25 St. Stephen's Green, Dublin 2, Ireland
Penguin Books India (P) Ltd, 11, Community Centre, Panchsheel Park, New Delhi – 110 017, India
Penguin Group (NZ), cnr Airborne and Rosedale Roads, Albany, Auckland 1310, New Zealand
Penguin Books (South Africa) (Pty) Ltd, 24 Sturdee Avenue, Rosebank 2196, South Africa

Penguin Group, Registered Offices: 80 Strand, London WC2R 0RL, England

First published in Viking Canada hardcover by Penguin Group (Canada),
a division of Pearson Penguin Canada Inc., 2002
Published in Penguin Canada paperback by Penguin Group (Canada),
a division of Pearson Penguin Canada Inc., 2003

2 3 4 5 6 7 8 9 10   (WEB)

Manufactured in Canada.

NATIONAL LIBRARY OF CANADA CATALOGUING IN PUBLICATION

Armstrong, Sally, 1943–
Veiled threat : the hidden power of the women of Afghanistan / Sally Armstrong.

Includes index.
ISBN 0-14-301281-9

1. Women—Afghanistan. 2. Women—Legal status, laws, etc.—Afghanistan.
3. Women—Afghanistan—Social conditions. I. Title.

HQ1735.6.A75 2003   305.4'09581   C2003-900898-3

American Library of Congress Cataloging in Publication data available

Visit the Penguin Group (Canada) website at www.penguin.ca

For the women of Afghanistan,
whose life journeys taught me the power
of struggle, courage and grace.

TABLE OF CONTENTS

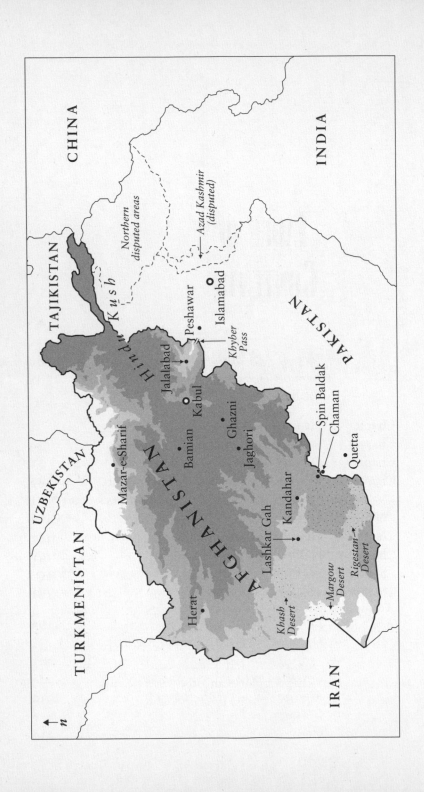

ACKNOWLEDGMENTS

When one is consumed with an assignment, as I was with the unfolding events in the lives of the women of Afghanistan, there are invariably a number of people who get caught like a tsunami in the surge of activity that comes with it. The storm around the women of Afghanistan kept changing. It went from bad to worse and then, after September 11, 2001, to the swirling winds of change. I need to thank the people who were the calm in my own storm, while I was on the odyssey of researching and writing this book: first, the publisher of Penguin Books, Cynthia Good, who suggested I write the book and gave me her unflagging support and encouragement; Diane Turbide, whose careful and precise editing of chapter after chapter after chapter made an otherwise complicated task a pleasure; and Dennis Mills, the copy editor, who managed to get his head around transliterations as well as grammar and had a charming way of telling me, "You already said that." And to Sandra Tooze, the senior production editor, my sincere thanks for shepherding this project, with hands-on precision and a brilliant final edit, to its date with the printer.

Researching the backdrop against which the women's lives were played was an immense challenge that was made easier by Antony Marcil, my hero of all things central Asian, whose own devotion to preserving the cultural integrity of this book was heaven-sent; by Linda Roan, my favorite Web aficionado, who connected me through cyberspace to sites around the world that were covering events in Afghanistan; and Marilou McPhedran, who bought a book I needed for research and gave it to me for Christmas—with a note promising to read it and highlight the information I needed. Now that's friendship. I also want to thank Mary McIver, Cheryl Embrett, Caroline Connell, Peter Carter and Tom Fennell, who edited the articles I wrote for *Homemaker's, Chatelaine* and *Maclean's* magazines, some of which I have referred to in this book; Jennifer Elliott, who chased down details I needed about Afghan history and delivered them to my home on her way to the hospital to deliver her third child; and, of course, Peter Bregg, the photo-journalism genius who sent me off with an idiot-proof camera and repeated patient lessons in photography before each assignment. I am grateful to Dr. Jamal Badawi and Reverend Jim McKnight, who helped me to understand the role religion plays in the lives of women.

Along the way I met people who influenced me enormously and whose help and advice made my work possible. Adeena Niazi and the women at the Afghan Women's Organization in Toronto were a valuable resource for information when I began researching in 1996, and they became wonderful friends while we worked together to bring awareness of the plight of their sisters in Afghanistan. Mohammad Azeem Besharat sat with me on a balcony in Kabul on a frosty winter day and brought a young poet's life into focus for me. His descriptions of that young woman, whose story is 1600 years old, confirmed my belief in the passion Afghan people have for their culture and history. Jennifer Jackman from the Feminist Majority Foundation in the U.S.; Janice Eisenhauer of Women for Women in Afghanistan, in Canada; and Farida Shaheed of Shirkat Gah, in Pakistan, kindly provided—by return e-mail— pieces of information I needed to tell the story about the women's groups around the world who stayed on the file to free the women in Afghanistan. And Hafeez Yaqoobi was always available to help me figure out a way to get into the country—and sometimes, how to get out—and was generous with his time as well as his expertise. The family of Dr. Sima Samar, particularly her half brother Ahmad Ali, made me feel welcome and shared their stories and anxieties about their beloved Afghanistan.

On the list of those I could never thank enough are Sima Samar, a rare bead on the world's scanty string of humanitarians. She's a woman whose moral courage and tenacity never failed to humble me, a woman whose friendship I treasure. And the wonderful women I met along the way from Kabul to Kandahar and Quetta to Peshawar—the women who shared their stories, their pain, their bravery and then had the grace to give me their friendship.

And last but never least, my family, who had to endure "the book." My children Heather, Peter and Anna, who were available 24/7 with advice, encouragement and love (not to mention take-out food) while I "booked" into the night. And their father, my husband of thirty-two years, whom we lost in a tragic accident on January 28, 2000. Ross encouraged me to stay with this story from the time I returned home with the first terrible news about the lives of women and girls in Afghanistan, and long before September 11, which ironically was his birthday.

To all, my heartfelt thanks.

INTRODUCTION

In March 1997 I flew halfway around the world to find a woman whose name I didn't know. Five and a half months earlier, the Taliban, a fundamentalist Islamic group, had taken control of Afghanistan and effectively put all women under house arrest. I had heard that one woman was working against the Taliban, trying to keep health clinics and schools open for women and girls, but no one would give me her name. Some women activists suggested I contact human-rights specialist Farida Shaheed in Lahore, Pakistan. My call to Shaheed produced more intrigue: "Come to Lahore and we'll discuss this," she offered.

I spent an entire day with Shaheed, picking up the ABCs of militant fundamentalism and wondering when I'd learn the name of the woman I wanted to see. "It's not safe to give out her name; she could be killed," explained Shaheed. Just before her office closed that day, she said, "Fly to Quetta [a city seven hundred kilometers (435 miles) to the west] tomorrow morning. Someone will meet you at the airport."

By the time the plane landed, my curiosity was thoroughly piqued. When I walked into the arrival lounge, a woman approached me, smiling, extending her hand and said, "You must be Sally. I'm Sima Samar. I believe you've been looking for me."

For the next ten days, I listened to her story as I followed her around the hospitals and schools she operates for women and girls. I discovered that she is the quintessential Afghan woman: she's strong, she adores her country, and she's had to fight for everything she's ever had. That day, when we settled into the car for the drive to Shuhada, her non-government organization in Quetta, she said, "I have three strikes against me. I'm a woman, I speak for women, and I'm Hazara—one of the most persecuted tribes in Afghanistan."

Sima Samar was only twelve years old when she learned the meaning of what author Rohinton Mistry would later write: "Life is poised as a fine balance between hope and despair." At that tender age, she began to fight to alter the status of women and girls in her country. She fought the suffocating rules in her own family. She fought the Soviets, the mujahideen, the Taliban. She fought every step of the way—to get an education and become a physician, to open her hospitals and schools for girls in Quetta and in Afghanistan, to raise her children according to her own values. Today thousands of girls in Afghanistan are educated because of Dr. Samar, and thousands of women have regained their health at her gentle and precise physician's hand. To the women and girls of Afghanistan, she is a hero. To the Taliban, who threatened to kill her for her refusal to cave in to their edicts, she was anathema. Once, when they told her to close her schools for girls or face death, she replied, "Go ahead and hang me in a public place. Then tell the people my crime: I was giving papers and pencils to the girls."

Today the hated Taliban is in tatters, and Sima Samar has returned to her beloved Afghanistan as deputy prime minister in charge of women's affairs. On December 4, 2001, when she was in Canada receiving the John Humphrey Freedom Award for the extraordinary work she'd done for Afghan women and girls, her son, Ali, called her at 4:30 a.m. "Mom, I'm watching BBC," he told her. "You've just been named to the interim government as one of five deputy prime ministers."

The task Dr. Samar faces is enormous. Her country is riven by brutal tribal disputes, and militant mullahs have inflicted countless human-rights abuses on her people. There is no infrastructure left, and on the day the new interim government took office, there was no electricity in Kabul, the capital city. People were starving, a measles epidemic that had begun in 2000 continued, and polio was running rampant. The schools had been closed for five years, and the few health clinics that still operated were damaged. Her six-month term to try to rebuild Afghanistan began on December 22, 2001.

I began to follow the story of the women of Afghanistan in 1996. When I read of the edicts the new Taliban regime had issued governing the lives of women and girls, I wanted to know how such a human-rights catastrophe could take place under the noses of the entire world. Initially, I anticipated that the assignment would require traveling to the region, interviewing the women, gathering the facts about the Taliban— how they got into power, how the international community were ignoring the plight of the women, and how the women were coping with the draconian decrees they were now forced to live with—and simply returning to Canada to write the article. However, in the process of researching the story, I came to know these women, their kindness, their humbling honesty and the brutal facts of their lives.

I finished the article in late March 1997, but I realized that I hadn't finished with the story. I had promised the women I met that I would try to raise awareness of their plight. And I had vowed, to myself, to try to find funds for Dr. Sima Samar's Shuhada organization, so that women and girls could get the health care they needed and the education they wanted in her clandestine clinics and schools.

After the article appeared (in *Homemaker's* magazine, where I was editor-in-chief at the time), more than nine thousand Canadian women wrote to me and demanded that something be done for these women. What followed were five fascinating, troubling, frustrating and rewarding years of reporting on the women of Afghanistan and working with women around the world to raise awareness as well as funds, to pressure the power-brokers into considering the women caught in this calamity, and ultimately to witness the collapse of the Taliban regime. As well, I saw two women, Dr. Sima Samar and Dr. Suhaila Seddiqi, appointed to the cabinet of the interim government, one as minster of women's affairs, the other as minister of health.

On January 27, 2002, an e-mail from Pamela Collett in Venezuela traveled through cyberspace to the thousands of women the world over who'd been connected to one another through the struggle. She said, "We should all join hands and shout for joy that our work has helped create an opening for Afghan women to struggle for their human rights to be included in the long-term process of establishing profound peace and security for all in Afghanistan. Together we made it possible. Thousands of us around the world, each in her own way, within her circle of friends and colleagues, have been working to ensure the women of Afghanistan were not forgotten. We did not give up, despite the opposition of the U.S. State Department, Pakistan's Intelligence Services, extremist religious groups operating under the title 'Islamists,' transnational energy companies such as Unocal, and other formidable foes. Women and girls in Afghanistan and the refugee camps in Pakistan have always been the true heroines who struggled to keep their humanity despite all the forces arrayed against them."

In February 2002, I went back to Afghanistan to find those heroic women, the ones I'd interviewed during their five-year battle for survival under the Taliban. My voyage began in Kabul, at Sima Samar's new home, and extended to Kandahar, where only one year earlier I'd met secretly with women in the basement of a building and listened to their horror stories about life under the Taliban. So much had changed. My heroes in this five-year odyssey were filled with hope and energy for the future. They were keenly aware of the pitfalls on the road ahead but steadfastly determined to overcome the abuses of the past and to create a future for their daughters.

In the process, I learned more than I ever could have imagined. In 1997 I had set out to find a woman whose name I didn't know. In the months and years that followed, I learned about Islam, about the history of this awesome country of Afghanistan and about the tribal mix that has been the root of so much of its conflict. I felt the generosity and hospitality of the Afghan people. I witnessed their extraordinary pride and passion in their country, as well as their amazing struggle to survive and their relentless refusal to be governed by outsiders. But mostly, I learned about the women—the way their lives are yoked to culture and religion, their courageous convictions about the role they played in the history of Afghanistan, their bravery and moxie in facing the future, and the road they feel they must travel in their quest for peace.

This is their story.

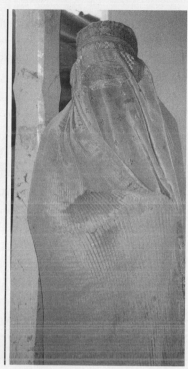

Chapter 1

HOUSE ARREST

It's curious that the sun was shining on the morning the women of Afghanistan were plunged into the Dark Ages. September 27, 1996, was a brilliant fall day in Kabul. Hamida Omid, the principal of the Ashia Droni High School who doubles as a radio announcer for the kids' afternoon show, remembers the eerie quiet that morning. She knew there could be trouble—she, her husband and four children had heard the rumbling of Taliban tanks the night before. They'd heard what the Taliban had done to women in Kandahar, where they'd taken power two years earlier. They knew that this ragtag band of bandits—mostly illiterate young men in their twenties—had a hateful policy toward women, putting them under virtual house arrest. When the loudspeaker on the mosque near her home came on and a shrieking voice announced loathsome rules for women, she knew she was listening to the voice of evil. What she didn't know was the diabolical shape it would take in the days and years to come—and that it would be delivered in the name of God.

"Women will stay at home," the mullah raged. "Women will not work," he continued. Hamida caught her breath. What about her job? If she didn't work, how would they eat? Her husband, an engineer, hadn't had work in years, as the city had limped from one political and economic crisis to the next. Now the mullah was decreeing that schools for girls would be closed immediately. What about her daughters? she wondered. That was just the beginning. Health clinics were also to be closed to women and girls. There would be no television, no radio, no singing, dancing, clapping, no kite flying, no toys for children— the list seemed endless.

Then they announced that a woman could only leave her home if she had a permit giving her a reason to be outside. Even then, she could only leave if she was accompanied by a man—her husband, father, brother or son. Moreover, she had to be wrapped head to foot in a burqa, a tent-like garment that fits tightly over the head, flows to the ankles, and has only a rectangle of mesh for the woman to look through. The burqa (or chadori, as most women call it) became the coup de grâce for the women of Kabul; most of them had never owned a burqa, and now that their means of earning money had been annulled, they would be forced to buy one at a cost of 200,000 Afghani (about $10). Taliban leader Mullah Mohammed Omar said flatly, "A woman's face corrupts men."

Until that day, women had made up 70 percent of Afghanistan's teachers, 50 percent of the civil service, 40 percent of the doctors, half the students at Kabul University, and had worked in the government as cabinet ministers and members of parliament. Now they were invisible.

Hamida had never worn or even owned a burqa. She dashed to her neighbor's house, borrowed a burqa and ran to check on her school. The sight in the street was shocking: cars belonging to rival mujahideen factions (who'd been fighting for control of the city for the previous four years) had been burned; the Taliban tanks that had rolled into Kabul had taken up positions on the main roads; the shops were all closed. The city where she'd grown up, attended university and launched her career was like a ghost town. The downtown was worse. The government leaders had been hanged—their bloated, beaten bodies still swinging from a traffic-light post in the public square (outside the presidential palace near the UN compound) so that city residents could witness the fate of the last Soviet-backed leaders. The Taliban had placed cigarettes between the fingers of the bodies and stuffed money in their shirt pockets. Mohammad Najibullah and his brother Shahpur Ahmadzai had been castrated, beaten and shot during the night, then hung from steel-wire nooses. When Hamida reached the high school, Taliban guards surrounded her, demanding to know why she was out of the house, and threatening her with jail if she dared to leave her home again without a permit and in the company of a male relative. Hamida felt that her world had gone mad. Stumbling through the streets in the cumbersome burqa, she wondered how she and her family would manage, what would become of them.

Wahida Nader, a supervisor at Save the Children in Kabul, borrowed a burqa and went to work that day. Under the burqa she was wearing jeans, a T-shirt and make-up, as well as nail polish. She was only a few blocks away from home when the Taliban's religious police (who called themselves "the

Department of the Enforcement of Right Islamic Way and Prevention of Evil") stopped her. "They beat me with a long rubber stick when they saw my nail polish," she says. "I'd decided no one would have that kind of control over me, and I was going to keep wearing it. But just behind me they stopped a young woman, a bride who still had her manicure from her wedding ceremony. They held her hands down on the road and cut off her fingertips. She lost her mind after that."

On the other side of the city, Fatana Osman, a psychiatrist who worked with children at Oxfam's city project, remembers that day. "On September 26, we were at work," says Fatana. "Everyone was anxious. The Taliban were near the city. We were waiting for something bad. At noon most people went home because we could hear the shelling. We'd heard about Taliban policies and we were afraid for our futures."

The next morning they heard about the fate of the government leaders on the radio—and they heard the Taliban's misogynist manifesto for women. "I'd never owned a burqa in my life," said Fatana. "Most women in Kabul had never even worn a scarf over their heads."

Her friend, Mina Ali, who was working as a pharmacist until that day, added, "These were strange rules for our country. They are not Islamic. It's power under the name of religion. And it was very hard for people. They didn't have any money for food, so where would they get money to buy a burqa?"

Fatana recalled the physical and psychological effects she felt when she had to wear a burqa. "It was hot. Shrouded in this body bag, I felt claustrophobic. It was smelly, too. The cloth in front of my mouth was damp from my breathing. Dust from the filthy street swirled up under the billowing burqa and stuck to the moisture from my covered mouth. I felt like I was suffocating in stale air.

"It also felt like I was invisible. No one could see me. No one knew whether I was smiling or crying. The mesh opening didn't give me enough view to see where I was going. It was like wearing horse blinders. I could see only straight in front of me. Not above or below or on either side of the path. Suddenly, when the road changed, I stepped on the edge of the hideous bag that covered my body and tumbled to the ground. No one helped me. It felt like no one in the world wanted to help the women."

For women, Afghanistan had become the equivalent of a medieval insane asylum, a place where mothers and wives, sisters and daughters were seen as a threat to holiness. The noose strung up by the Taliban tightened daily. In the absence of any real protest from the international community, a litany of new rules followed: photographs, even ones taken at wedding ceremonies, were considered un-Islamic; so were sports for girls. White socks, the only item of clothing that shows beneath the burqa, were forbidden; the reason given was that white is the color of the Taliban flag. Make-up, nail polish and high-heeled shoes were taboo. They ordered female patients to leave the hospitals, since the staff included male doctors. Female staff were also dismissed.

In the subsequent days and weeks, the Taliban leader, Mullah Mohammed Omar, issued more edicts. When women walked to the bazaar to find food and water for their families, their feet could make no noise; they had to wear wedged shoes and walk silently. Hamida soon found out that she wasn't even allowed to speak to her husband when they walked together to the bazaar. Windows had to be painted over to prevent anyone from seeing a woman inside the house. New houses could have no windows on the second floor. Women were forbidden to ride in the front seat of a car. They had to sit in the back and be screened by curtains drawn around the windows and across the front seat. In a stupefying rationale, Omar explained the Taliban's actions against women by saying, "Otherwise they'll be like Lady Diana."

One woman went to the butcher to buy meat for her family and let her hand show while she was passing the money to the clerk. The Taliban guards dragged her outside the shop and beat her severely. Another woman who dared to wear high-heeled shoes was beaten as well. When she cried out for mercy, they beat her again for making a noise. The women in Kabul were wearing a lot more than day dresses under their burqas; they were hiding ugly bruises from the beatings inflicted for trivial reasons every time they came in contact with the Taliban. Hamida says the Taliban would even board the mini-buses that transported women to dispense impromptu beatings.

Under Taliban rule, Kabul's 30,000 widows became virtually destitute. Many of their husbands had died in the civil war that had been raging for seventeen years. Now they couldn't leave their homes, they couldn't work, they couldn't even go to the bazaar to beg for food for their children. When asked how they should cope, the women said the Taliban replied, "Let them die." Some men even told their disabled wives that they no longer required a prosthesis since they no longer needed to be seen outside.

I traveled to the region soon after the Taliban took over. I wanted to find out how the women were coping and to try to determine what it was the Taliban were trying to accomplish. When I asked an official in the Taliban administration office in Quetta, Pakistan, to explain the brutalization of women, he dismissed my inquiry with contempt and said I was overreacting. "We stoned a few bad women to death and every prostitute left the city. We were efficient. No one else could get rid of those women." The fact that there was no trial, no rule of law and no judiciary didn't faze the official in the least. The women soon came to understand the Taliban style: It's my word against yours. I have the gun. You are only a woman.

Not that life under the mujahideen had been much better. While the mujahideen fought each other for power, from 1992 until 1996, the streets of Kabul and Kandahar were notoriously perilous. Women were being raped in broad daylight, and robberies had become as common as shopping. But the Taliban legitimized the misogyny. The women in Kabul had heard the story about a woman in Kandahar: she was being taken to the hospital for the delivery of her child when a gang of Taliban soldiers stopped the car. When they learned the woman was about to give birth, they said they wanted to see how a baby was born and took her to their leader's house. The woman labored for hours on her own while they stood and watched. She finally delivered the baby, but the child died minutes later because no one knew how to resuscitate an infant who had failed to start breathing on its own. The Taliban marched the woman to the door where her husband waited and told him to take her and the dead baby to the hospital.

To disobey the Taliban was to die. Soon after the takeover, a group of women in the city of Herat marched in protest. According to eyewitnesses, the Taliban surrounded the women, seized the leader, doused her in kerosene and burned her alive. Women were sprayed with acid, beaten with twisted wires and shot for crimes such as showing their ankles, letting a hand slip from under the burqa while paying for food or allowing their children to play with toys. As for being outside with any man who was not a relative, the sentence was death by stoning. On Fridays, the holy day, these sentences were carried out in what used to be the soccer stadium in Kabul or in the Hall of Honor in Kandahar. In other cities, any public gathering place was used, and the local people were forced to attend the executions. The men in power would dig a pit and bury the woman to her shoulders or toss her to the ground, tie her hands and feet together and cover her with her burqa. Then they would form a circle around her and throw rocks at her head until she was dead. The Taliban's edict said that the rocks thrown must not be so big as to kill her quickly.

The Taliban justified their actions in the name of Islam. But Muslim scholars all over the world have condemned their actions, arguing that they have nothing to do with Islam. It was a grab for power and control in a country that had been struggling with unrest for eighteen years. It was also a dreadfully misogynist interpretation of Islam, based on a contempt for women that marks the disturbing rise in extremism in countries all over the world. In Bangladesh, a woman can receive fifty lashes for speaking her mind. In Pakistan, a rape victim can be jailed for fornication. In Saudi Arabia, women are forced to cloak themselves in black chadors, which absorb the stifling heat, while men walk about in white robes, which deflect it. In 1996 Afghanistan followed with its own set of human-rights violations.

Astonishingly, this throwback to a medieval era created a strange wall of silence. While the United Nations wrung its hands, government leaders the world over looked the other way. The women of Afghanistan were left feeling like the living dead and wondering who, in the name of Allah, had decreed this miserable fate for them.

In the early days, some Afghans dared to hope the Taliban would bring peace to the country, that they'd take the guns away and get rid of the lawless mujahideen. There had been rumors they'd bring back King Zahir Shah, who'd been in exile in Rome since the overthrow of the monarchy in 1973. Some said the Taliban had no interest in taking power and only wanted to establish stability in the country. Many were willing to sacrifice the human rights of women and girls to gain peace. But it quickly became apparent that no one had rights under the Taliban. While the war on women started immediately, men and children soon began to suffer under the Taliban's rules. Children were beaten for flying kites. Men without beards were fired from their jobs and jailed for wearing Western clothing. Those with long hair were arrested and had their heads shaved.

While television was banned and the TV station in Kabul was shut down, the sets remained in peoples' homes until the

Taliban found out that citizens were using satellite dishes to watch news and video movies. Authorities began raiding homes, seizing television sets and impaling them on street poles. Wahida Nader says everyone knew they kept the color sets for themselves. Hypocrisy was the hallmark of the Taliban. "Still, we found ways to keep televisions hidden, to keep satellite dishes working," she says. "We watched BBC and CNN—news became as important as food."

For the women of Afghanistan, life under the Taliban was like nature thrown into reverse. They were like spring blossoms forced to fold their beautiful petals back into their casings. With downcast eyes and sagging shoulders, the young women I met described their grievances in words that made me think of a line from the poem "In Flanders Fields": "Short days ago we lived." They had attended university in Kabul, worn jeans and short skirts, met at the restaurants on Da Afghanan, and gone to discos on Froshga. Like other young people, they had walked along the river and through Pul bagh Vuumi Park with their friends. Their lives were full, their futures hopeful—despite the fact their country had been unstable since the 1979 Soviet invasion.

But the forces that rid the country of communism in 1992 had set up an internecine war right in the heart of their city. Extremist factions had fought each other for control for four deadly years before the ultra-extremist Taliban won and seized power in autumn of 1996. And women like Fatana and Mina, as well as Hamida and Wahida, became invisible. Their jobs, social lives and self-esteem disappeared overnight.

When I asked Fatana in early March of 1997 what effect this had on the mental health of the women, her friend Farahnaz Mehdiz, a civil engineer, spoke up. "I can answer that question for you. It's six months since the Taliban arrived, and I don't want to leave my house. I start to laugh or cry and I don't know why. I feel sad all the time. And I cannot concentrate. The other day I was helping someone with accounting and I realized I'd

entered the same number over and over again. I have no hope
for my future, and what's worse, I have no hope for the future
of my two children."

No wonder. The streets of Kabul were like a moonscape: shops
and restaurants closed, 60 percent of the city destroyed, roads full
of holes, garbage everywhere, no electricity in most parts of the
city and almost no running water. When the university reopened
a few months later, only boys could attend. Women doctors
were allowed to return to work later in 1997 but only to treat
women patients. The hospital they were assigned to work in had
no electricity or running water, but it had a menacing Taliban
guard at the door. When one woman arrived with burns to
three-quarters of her body, the doctor began to remove her
burqa but the Taliban guard said it was not allowed. "If I don't
remove the burqa, she will die," the doctor told the guard. He
refused permission. The woman died shortly afterwards.

By 1996 the world had clearly grown weary of Afghanistan
and its eighteen years of conflict. Theirs was now the forgotten
war. After the king was overthrown in 1973, Afghanistan had
become a republic and had made considerable advances
toward modernization. But the Soviet Union invaded in 1979
and threw the country into chaos—in what became the last
violent crucible of the Cold War. For ten years, the mujahideen
(or freedom fighters, as the anti-communist West called them)
struggled to rid the country of the Soviets. When the Russians
pulled out in 1989, President Najibullah struggled to stay in
power until 1992, when he was overthrown by the mujahideen.
But then, the seven different factions of the mujahideen began
a fratricidal bloodbath as they vied for power. Life became
more violent than it had been under the Soviets and more
religiously strict than the people had ever imagined. One of
those factions, the Taliban, emerged victorious.

The people trapped in the country—and the 500,000 refugees
who had escaped to border towns in northern Pakistan—were

hoping someone would "take up our quarrel with the foe." But the Islamic Republic of Pakistan, along with Saudi Arabia and the United Arab Emirates, recognized the Taliban and gave them embassy status. The black-turbaned bullies had been strutting around the refugee camps in Pakistan's border cities of Quetta and Peshawar ever since they had taken over Kandahar in 1994, threatening those who had managed to escape the country. As well, the steady rise in fundamentalism in Pakistan left many refugees in this northern region wary. Many women continued to wear a burqa out of fear. Others were careful to cover up just to avoid attention from the extremists. There was an uneasy calm.

Among the refugees in Quetta was an Afghan woman physician who had been thumbing her nose at the fundamentalists by providing education and health care to the women and girls. A few days before September 27, she traveled through Kabul to the northern Afghan city of Mazar-e-Sharif. She was there to help the people who'd fled to that city when the Taliban gained control of Kandahar and Herat. The Taliban knew her and despised her for her bold refusal to bow to their edicts. So when the news hit Mazar-e-Sharif that the Taliban had taken the capital, she knew she dared not return via Kabul. Instead, she hitched a lift on a United Nations plane back to Quetta. Little did she know, while she contemplated the trials her people would face under Taliban rule, that five years later she would return to Kabul as the deputy prime minister of a new, post-Taliban government. Dr. Sima Samar's five-year struggle with the Taliban became legend to the women and girls she served and to people the world over.

The Edicts

When the Taliban renamed the country the Islamic Emirate of Afghanistan, they issued new edicts regularly. Most of these were directed at women, which meant any female who looked as if she had reached puberty and was often interpreted as being any girl over the age of eight. The edicts proclaimed that a woman must be totally covered, including her face, whenever she left her home. She was subject to a host of draconian laws that, at best, kept her behind a purdah wall and denied her participation in society; at worst, she was sent to the infamous Hall of Honor, where public punishments included flogging, hanging or stoning to death for alleged impropriety.

The following three edicts, the first of hundreds that followed, are a verbatim translation by United Nations staff.

Edict Number One—Notice of Department for Enforcement of Right Islamic Way and Prevention of Evils:

The Department for Enforcement of Right Islamic Way and Prevention of Evils for the Implementation of legal Islamic orders and Prophet Mohamed [*sic*] tradition in order to prevent evils which cause serious dangers and problems for Islamic society requests from all Pious sisters and brothers to seriously follow 8 articles mentioned below to prevent occurrence of evils:

1. No exit and traveling of sisters without escort of legal close relatives (Mahram).
2. Those sisters are coming out of their homes with legal escort should use veil (burqa) or similar things to cover the face.
3. Sitting of sisters in the front seat of cart (gadi) and Jeep (vehicle) without legal relative is forbidden. In the case of appearance, serious measures will be carried out against the vehicle and cart rider/driver.
4. Shop keepers do not have right to buy or sell things with those women without covered face, otherwise the shop keeper is guilty and has no right to complain.

5. Cars are strictly forbidden to be covered with flowers for wedding ceremony and also is not allowed to drive around the city.
6. Women's invitations in hotels and wedding party in hotels are forbidden.
7. Sisters without legal close relative with them cannot use taxis, otherwise the taxi driver is responsible.
8. The person who is in charge of collecting fares (money) for sisters in buses, mini-buses and jeeps should be under 10 years old.

The professional delegates of this department are in charge to punish violators according to Islamic principles.

Edict Number Two—Taliban Islamic Movement of Afghanistan Rules of Work for the State Hospitals and Private Clinics based on Shari'a principles:

1. Female patients should go to see female physicians. In case a male physician is needed, the female patient should be accompanied by her close relatives (Mahram).
2. During examination, the female patients and male physicians both should be dressed with an Islamic Hijab.
3. Male physicians should not touch or see the other parts of female patients except the affected part.
4. Waiting rooms for female patients should be safely covered.
5. The person who regulates turns for female patients should be a female.
6. During night duty, in rooms where female patients are hospitalized, a male doctor without the call of patient is not allowed to enter the room.
7. Sitting and speaking between male and female doctors are not allowed. If there be need for discussion, it should be done with Hejab [*sic*].

8. Female doctors should wear simple clothes, they are not allowed to wear stylish clothes or use cosmetics and make-up.
9. Female doctors and nurses are not allowed to enter the room where male patients are hospitalized.
10. Hospital staff should pray in the mosque on time. The Director of Hospital is bound to assign a place and appoint a priest (mullah) for prayer.
11. Staff of (Amri Bel Maroof Wa Nai Az Munkar) religious police department are allowed to go for control at any time and nobody can prevent them. Anybody who violates the order will be punished as per Islamic regulations.

Signed
Amirul-Mominin Mullah Mohammad Omer Mujhahed and Mofti Mohammad Masoom Afghani (Acting Minister of Public Health).

Edict Number Three—Islamic State of Afghanistan
General Presidency of Amri Bel Maroof Wa Nai Az Munkar
(Religious Police)
Administration Department

To the received letter from the cultural and social affairs department of General Presidency of Islamic States of Afghanistan no. 6240 dated 26. 09. 1375 [December 16, 1996] states that:
The role and regulation of Amri Bel Maroof Wa Nai Az Munkar (Religious Police) is to be distributed via your office to all whom it may concern for implementation.

1. To prevent sedition and uncovered females (be hejab): no drivers are allowed to pick up females who are using Iranian burqa. In the case of violation the driver will be

imprisoned. If such kinds of female are observed in the street, their houses will be found and their husbands punished. If the woman use stimulating and attractive cloth and there is no close male relative with them the drivers should not pick them up.

2. To prevent music: to be broadcasted by the public information resources. In shops, hotels, vehicles and rickshaws cassettes and music are prohibited. This matter should be monitored within five days. If any music cassette is found in a shop, the shopkeeper should be imprisoned and the shop locked. If five people guarantee, the shop could be opened and the criminal released later. If a cassette is found in a vehicle, the vehicle and the driver will be imprisoned. If five people guarantee, the vehicle will be released and the criminal released later.

3. To prevent beard shaving and its cutting: to be broadcasted by the public information resources. After one and a half months if anyone is observed who has shaved and/or cut his beard, he should be arrested and imprisoned until his beard gets bushy.

4. To prevent not praying an order gathering prayer at the bazaar: to be broadcasted by the public information resources that the prayers should be done on their due times in all districts. The exact prayer time will be announced by the Amri Bel Maroof Wa Nai Az Munkar (religious police) department. Fifteen minutes prior to prayer time the front of the mosque, where the water facilities and possibilities are available, should be blocked and transportation should be strictly prohibited and all people are obliged to go to the mosque. At the prayer time, this matter should be monitored. If young people are seen in the shops they will be immediately imprisoned. If five people guarantee, the person should be released, otherwise the criminal will be imprisoned for 10 days.

5. To prevent keeping pigeons and playing with birds: to be broadcasted by the public information resources that within 10 days this habit/hobby should stop. After 10 days this matter should be monitored and the pigeons and any other playing birds should be killed.

6. To eradicate the use of addiction and its users: addicts should be imprisoned and investigation made to find the supplier and the shop. The shop should be locked and both criminals (the owner and the user) should be imprisoned and punished.

7. To prevent kite flying: first should be broadcasted by the public information resources advising the people of its useless consequences such as betting, death of children and their deprivation from education. The kite shops in the city should be abolished.

8. To prevent idolatry: to be broadcasted by the public information resources that in vehicles, shops, room, hotels, and any other places pictures/portraits should be abolished. The monitors should tear up all pictures in the above places. This matter should be announced to all transport representatives. The vehicle will be stopped if any idol is found in the vehicle.

9. To prevent gambling: in collaboration with the security police the main centre should be found and the gamblers imprisoned for one month.

10. To prevent British and American hairstyles: to be broadcasted by the public information resources that people with long hair should be arrested and taken to the Amri Bel Maroof Wa Nai Az Munkar (religious police) department to shave their hair. The criminal has to pay the barber.

11. To prevent interest charges on loans: charges on changing small denomination notes and charges on money orders: all money exchangers should be informed that the above three types of exchanging money are prohibited in Islam.

In the case of violation, the criminal will be imprisoned for a long time.

12. To prevent washing clothes by young ladies along the water streams in the city: it should be announced in all mosques and the matters should [be] monitored. Violator ladies should be picked up with respectful Islamic manner, taken to their houses and their husbands severely punished.

13. To prevent music and dances in wedding parties: to be broadcasted by the public information resources that the above two things should be prevented. In the case of violation the head of the family will be arrested and punished.

14. To prevent the playing of music drums: first the prohibition of this action to be announced to the people. If anybody does this then the religious elders can decide about it.

15. To prevent sewing ladies' cloth and taking female body measures by tailor: if women or fashion magazines are seen in the shop the tailor should be imprisoned.

16. To prevent sorcery: all the related books should be burnt and the magician should be imprisoned until his repentance.

The above issues are stated and you are requested, according to your job responsibilities, to implement and inform your related organizations and units.

Signed: Mawlavi Enayatullah Baligh
Deputy Minister
General Presidency of Amri Bel Maroof Wa Nai Az Munkar
The Religious Police

Chapter 2

SIMA SAMAR:
THE DOCTOR
IS IN

She's a storyteller. Whether kibitzing with her patients at her hospital clinic in Quetta or explaining the status of women in Afghanistan to President George Bush in the White House, Sima Samar has a way of making her point with a raconteur's talent, an historian's adroitness and a humorist's gift of understatement. I'd only known her for a few days when I began to look forward to the body language that prefaced an anecdote. Her eyes begin to twinkle, a droll smile spreads across her face, her long slender fingers slap her thigh and she begins with, "You know . . ." What follows is invariably a history lesson laced with humor and common sense. It's a skill she's used effectively for most of her life.

19

The road Sima Samar traveled from Jaghori (in the province of Ghazni), where she was born, to the refugee centre in Quetta, where we first met, is strewn with the history and customs of Afghanistan, the country she once said she'd give her life for. Her father, Qadam Ali Yaqubi, had two wives, not an unusual practice for Muslim men—the Koran allows four wives. But it's a custom Sima doesn't approve of. She was only six years old, the third child of the first wife, when she realized that her mother, Khurshid, was being treated unfairly because she was the first wife. The two wives not only lived together, but slept in the same bed. Sima was close in age to the second-born of the second wife's nine children. The two babies slept between the two women and were breast-fed by both of them. But as Sima grew, she saw the humiliation and the torment her mother had to endure. "I thought it wasn't right," she recalls.

Young Sima's world changed when her father, who'd been a civil servant in the government, left for Lashkar Gah in the province of Helmand, about 600 kilometers (370 miles) away, where he had bought land. He started a sheep farm, taking the second wife and her children with him and leaving five-year-old Sima and her brother and sister behind in the care of their mother and uncles.

Sima was precocious: she knew that the best food was always given to the men and then to the sons, but she managed to convince her uncles to give it to her. "I was naughtier than the other kids," she says. I broke most of the rules. But I got away with it."

She was six when she traveled with her mother, brother and sister, Aziza, to Lashkar Gah for a visit. They weren't supposed to stay, but her father decided the two families should be together; since his word was law, her mother, who'd been happy living in Jaghori had no say in the matter. He enrolled Sima at the co-educational school in Lashkar Gah, where she learned her first painful lesson in ethnic hatred. Her father explained to the headmistress that his daughter could already read at the grade one level and that she should be placed in grade two. They put her in grade two, but reading in Pashtun was different from the Persian language she was used to. It led to her first confrontation. "Many Hazaras are Shi'ite Muslims," she explains. "The Pashtuns are Sunni Muslims. When I was asked to name a holy man in class, I said 'Ali.' The Pashtuns say 'char yar ba safa,' which means the four pure men. The teacher called me a stupid Hazara." Little Sima was devastated. "I was crying. The teacher took me to the headmistress who said, 'When you're at home you can say Ali, but at school you must not.'

"I wanted to go home but didn't know how to get there. While I waited for my brother to come and fetch me, I thought of ways to avoid ever returning to that school." The next day her father took her back, and Sima was moved to another classroom. But although she'd scored a victory in escaping the teacher who had insulted her, there was no escaping the hurtful truth that she had been singled out because of her ethnic origins. It was a lesson she'd remember the rest of her life.

When she was seven, she learned another painful lesson. Her sister, Aziza, had been promised in marriage to a cousin. Aziza said she'd rather be killed than marry this man. "She was seventeen years old," says Sima. "I remember seeing my mother drag her by her hair to the room where our cousin waited. She forced Aziza to marry him. It left a very big impression on me." She knew her sister was miserable in her marriage, and her misery was made worse by the fact that she didn't get pregnant. "Everyone was after her. They were so mean to her." A few years later, Aziza got sick and died of meningitis at the age of twenty-one. Before she died, though, Aziza had given Sima advice. "Study hard," she said. "Education is the only escape from this way of living."

Sima also began to understand the way women hidden behind purdah walls use power. "When I was in grade seven at school I was getting very good marks and my father gave me a hundred Afghanis to reward me. The second wife took herself to bed for a week. She said she was sick. But I knew it was her way of letting my father know that she disapproved of his attention to me."

Sima was a voracious reader. From Persian books she borrowed from friends, she learned that other people didn't live with the same strict rules that her family adhered to. By the time she was twelve, she knew she would rebel, that she could never accept the rules of the society she lived in. "The mullah was saying that a girl should be married before her first menses, that every menses was a crime because an ovum had been wasted. I knew I had to find a way to change this thinking or get out of there."

At fourteen, she secretly joined a Maoist party. "I was always looking for a solution. I tried praying, but I saw so many poor people, so many people who had nothing—and others who had everything. I was drawn to other people who wanted to make change. I wanted equality for men and women, for rich people and poor people. I felt it was wrong that some people couldn't afford to eat." There was an American agriculture project being conducted in Helmand province, and the high school she attended had hired American Peace Corps teachers. Her school was co-educational; it didn't have the ubiquitous boundary wall. She played basketball and soccer on the school fields and went to movies with her friends. She ran along the riverbanks, climbed trees and ignored the stifling rules for girls.

In 1975 she graduated from high school and won a scholarship to study in Australia and another one to study in Hungary. But rigid custom had caught up with her: her father said an unmarried daughter could not leave home and he forbade her to accept the scholarships. She had also been accepted at Kabul University, but again, her father refused to allow her to leave.

When she suggested she could stay at the student hostel on the campus, he was horrified at the notion. But Sima was adamant about going to university, so when her father offered to arrange a marriage for her, she reluctantly agreed. She saw it was the only way she could realize her dream and escape the suffocating life in Lashkar Gah.

The husband her father selected was Abdul Ghafoori Sultani, a thirty-year-old physics professor at Kabul University. The handsome, bearded Abdul was in love with his eighteen-year-old bride. Sima respected him and enjoyed his company and, after all, he'd been her escape route. But she wasn't in love with him. She speaks softly of the man who rescued her: "I was very fond of him. He was my friend. But I didn't need another man to oppress me. I needed a man to help me."

At Kabul University, Sima became more politicized. The king had been overthrown two years earlier, and the country was now a republic, led by Mohammad Daoud, who had developed close ties between Afghanistan and the Soviet Union to gain financial assistance. The opposition political party in Afghanistan, called Khalq, which means "the masses," was also pro-Russian and actively recruiting supporters for Soviet rule, a strategy Sima saw as disastrous. She and Abdul joined the resistance movement, handing out pamphlets describing the danger of Soviet invasion and attending street demonstrations against the communists. Sima also gave birth, on November 29, 1978, to their first child, a boy she and Abdul named Ali Qais.

Abdul and Sima knew the work they were doing to oust the Russian sympathizers was dangerous, but they persevered. "I would throw my papers [toss her political pamphlets to passersby] in the early morning and run off to classes," she says. She was in her third year of medical school in 1978 when the pro-Russian party, Khalq, overthrew the government, and Sima and Abdul went underground with their work. "You couldn't speak in public against the Russians or you would be

killed," she says. "The issue wasn't about religion, it was about
culture. While the Russian supporters said they were freeing
the women, in fact they were only freeing women to sing on a
stage or wear short skirts. Our human rights were never
advanced by them or the Russians." Indeed, the punishment
for those men who spoke against the Soviets was to be tied up
and forced to watch while a gang of communist sympathizers
raped their wives. Sima's own father came to Kabul to beat her
when he discovered she was working for the resistance.

Abdul worried constantly that their political activities and
his wife's outspokenness would lead to her being injured. Sima
took little Ali to Lashkar Gah to stay with her mother when the
situation worsened. A year later they paid the ultimate price for
defending their homeland against foreign influences. Sima was
working near Kabul in the mornings and attending classes in
the afternoon. She was on a bus traveling back to the center of
the city when she realized something terrible had happened.
There'd been a bombing and an outbreak of fighting in downtown Kabul. She hurried home and found a worried Abdul,
who'd decided it was necessary to get extra supplies—bread,
potatoes, onions—before the evening curfew, as they could be
trapped in the house for a week if the police prolonged their
dragnet.

He left with his young brother, Atah, just sixteen years old.
They were returning home when the soldiers of the Khalq
government surrounded them and grabbed Atah. Abdul knew
they would beat the boy, but he also thought they would bring
him home later. Sima and Abdul quickly hid the pamphlets
they'd been handing around the city, as well as the shotgun they
kept in the cupboard. Sima went to the kitchen to prepare
dinner and Abdul sat down to work on the examination he was
giving his students the next day. Together, they waited anxiously
for Atah to return. He did return, but the intimidation he'd
experienced at the hands of the police, who threatened to kill

him if he was involved in anti-government activity, heightened Abdul's concerns for Sima. She had spoken against the government often and in public. He tried to tell her how much danger she was in, that she had to be more careful.

But it wasn't Sima they were looking for when ten men, including a student of Abdul's, pushed open their door at 10 o'clock that same night. They strutted into the room and told Abdul to come with them. Sima offered them money; the student said, "Don't worry, he'll be back." She told Abdul to wear his heavy coat and boots, in case they kept him in jail, but again the student assured her nothing would happen to the professor. Sima was scared to death. She could hardly find her voice when she said to the leader, "I don't trust you. Many people have disappeared. Where are you taking my husband?" They searched the house, found nothing and marched Abdul out to the street. "The last thing he said to me was, 'Don't go looking for me,' and his eyes were pleading when he added, 'It is too dangerous for you.'"

Sima never saw him again. Like thousands of other women whose men had disappeared, she petitioned the government every day, stood at the gate of the government palace and asked where the prisoners were being kept. She stopped soldiers on the street to inquire where Abdul was being held and she waited for news. She went home each night with an aching heart and wondered how she would manage—alone, penniless and knowing that she was a target as well.

She never stopped working for the resistance movement and joined a group called Jabah Majahideen Mubarzin, which was led by Dr. Faiz Ahmed. His wife Meena created a women's wing of the group called the Revolutionary Association of the Women of Afghanistan, better known today as RAWA. Together they plotted the demise of the Soviets. Sima went to school by day and to secret meetings by night. They had pseudonyms—some of Sima's were Esmat and Asam and Nadia. The work they did was perilous and many of their members disappeared, as Abdul had. But they were undeterred. To rescue their country, they knew they had to get rid of the Soviets.

In the meantime, Sima used every contact she had to try to find out what happened to Abdul. Six months later, in December 1979, the Soviets invaded Afghanistan and toppled the government of Mohammad Taraki and installed their own leader, Babrak Karmal, as president. When the Russians left more than a decade later, they destroyed their files and burned all the papers. Sima knows Abdul was killed, but she was never able to discover who murdered him or where they left his body.

In 1979 Sima had just over two years left in her medical studies, a fourteen-month-old baby to care for and her commitment to resistance work. Against the odds, she managed to graduate, one of the few Hazara woman to become a doctor in Afghanistan. She did her required four-month service at Wazir Akbar Khan Hospital in Kabul, but she then had to make a life for herself and little Ali somehow. A single mother in Afghanistan was an unheard-of phenomenon. Her father insisted she come home and remarry. Sima wasn't about to give up her hard-won freedom to go back to servitude. However, she knew it wasn't safe for her to stay in Kabul and considered moving to rural Afghanistan to live with her in-laws in Ghazni—but only on a trial basis. "I was afraid they would think that they owned me. I couldn't live like that again," she says. The decision was almost made for her when her family found out that she was still handing out anti-government pamphlets in Kabul. "I had a hiding place in the hospital where I could stash my pamphlets. I'd pass them around on the street early in the morning before going to the public baths. When my brothers found out, they told my father. He started beating me and demanded that I come home and get married again." She refused. Twenty days later she packed up her few belongings, including the red-and-white polka-dot quilt with tiny embroidered flowers that had been a wedding gift, and a family photo of Abdul, Ali and herself. She put on a burqa, because the mujahideen forces (who were now fighting the Soviet government) were roaming the countryside in Ghazni and wouldn't tolerate an uncovered woman. She and her young son, Ali, took the bus to Jaghori in the province of Ghazni. Her father and brothers never said goodbye.

When Dr. Sima Samar opened her first medical clinic at her in-laws' home, all she had was a stethoscope and a blood-pressure cuff. She stayed three years and recalls, "I was happy because there was so much I could do to help the women, particularly with obstetrics and gynecology. No one had ever tried to help them before, and their needs were enormous. I wrote to a friend and asked her to send me medical books. I'd read about a disease in the morning and treat it in the afternoon." There were no roads in the area, so getting to her patients was often a challenge in itself. Occasionally someone would take her by car, but a donkey was the more usual transport. Most often she went on foot. Once, the family of a woman who had been in labor for three days sent a message to Sima and begged her to come. She walked three hours to get there. On another occasion, she saddled up a horse and rode twelve hours over the steep, rock-strewn mountains to treat a child who was sick with pneumonia. In the meantime, her life with Abdul's family was as rough-hewn as the landscape. They couldn't understand this woman who wanted to leave the family compound to go out into the world beyond. And when they saw her climbing trees to pluck fresh fruit from the upper branches, they were mortified. Her situation was further complicated by the fact that the local mujahideen outlawed schools because they thought the children would only be taught communism. When it was time for Ali to begin his formal education, she knew she had to part with him again and was heartbroken when she sent him back to live with her mother in Helmand. Ali was her solace, her reminder of Abdul and the life they were supposed to share together as professionals in Kabul. The little boy with his father's handsome face meant the world to Sima. When he left, her life was consumed by her work.

She became a folk hero to the people of Ghazni. Everyone knew of "Dr. Sima." She birthed their babies and cared for their elderly. She stitched up their wounds and soothed their pains. She taught them how to avoid illnesses and tried to convince the women to have fewer children. She says she learned as much as they did. "Practicing medicine in a rural district revealed the brutality of the lives of women, and that the lack of education was a direct cause of the turmoil the country was in." She vowed that some day she would do something about both conditions.

Near the end of 1984, Sima developed whooping cough, and despite the fact that the local population thought she could cure any ailment, she couldn't kick the persistent cough. She decided to travel to Pakistan to seek treatment, but the voyage was formidable. The roads were controlled alternately by mujahideen and Soviet troops. Both forbade travel. She hid by day and traversed the mountains by night. It took two days and two nights to get to the city of Quetta on the other side of the southwest border of Afghanistan. Once there, she discovered a burgeoning diaspora—Afghans who had fled the unstable conditions of their homeland. As well, she found a school for Ali. It felt like the next best thing to home. She was desperate to have her young son back with her and decided to find a job and stay in Quetta.

The dusty, rocky desert landscape that unfolds from the mountains here is similar to the refugees' native land. The miniature yellow wildflowers that push defiantly out of the scrubby soil grow like symbols of their struggle. Stark contrasts—mud houses and rented two-story homes, the delicious scent of fresh-baked naan bread from the bakeries, and the putrid stench from the latrines in the street, the fear and longing of the people—define life in the refugee center.

In Quetta, Sima Samar discovered that Afghan women didn't have many more rights in Pakistan than they did in Afghanistan. The hospitals in the refugee quarter were mostly for men. The maternity health clinic closed every day between noon and four o'clock. "I tried to explain to them that women in labor don't follow the clock, that they need someone to keep the clinic open in the afternoon because babies have a way of deciding themselves when they'll arrive. But no one wanted to make changes for the women."

She found a hospital that treated women as well as men and applied for a job. When they asked to see her medical certificate, she had to tell them she didn't have one. (It was common practice in Soviet run countries to deny certificates to professionals, so they could never leave the country to work elsewhere.) It proved to be a minor obstacle for a woman whose life had been a series of hurdles. She went to Peshawar, a Pakistan city where diplomas of all sorts were sold, and for 300 rupees (about $10 at the time) bought a medical diploma. "I told the hospital what I had done and they took me anyway."

With Ali enrolled in school and Sima working full-time at Inter Church Aid, a non-government organization, life took on a semblance of normalcy. But Sima couldn't ignore the thousands of Afghan refugees living in appalling conditions in Pakistan. She couldn't dismiss the women whose efforts to cope with and care for their children were hampered by conservative mullahs who forbade them to visit male doctors and harassed those who ventured from their homes to work or attend school. In 1989 she gave up the security of a staff position at the hospital and opened a non-government organization called Shuhada, which means martyr, and started to realize some of her lifelong goals—to educate the women and girls of Afghanistan and to look after their health needs. She depended on the international humanitarian community for most of the funds, and she charged a nominal fee to those refugees who could afford to pay for the services.

Sima started with a medical clinic and a school for girls in Quetta. Then she hired doctors, nurses and teachers inside Afghanistan and opened hospitals and schools there as well. She also applied to the United Nations to get wheat for the wheat-for-work program, and she started paying her staff with food rather than the money she didn't have. The news of her work spread around the refugee camps like a flash fire. Hundreds of girls flocked to her schools, and the line-up at her clinic stretched out into the street. She tapped every international aid organization she could find for the funds to operate Shuhada, all the while hoping it was a temporary solution and that they'd all be able to go home as soon as the Soviets left Afghanistan. She started sewing and quilting projects so the women could earn money. An excellent stitcher herself, she guided them through the patterns and insisted that the work meet her own high standards. In the meantime, her steadfast refusal to observe purdah—and the stand she took on equality for women—made her anathema to the fundamentalists, but a hero to the women she was serving.

But religious fundamentalism was spreading rapidly and menacingly. The mujahideen who roamed the countryside in Afghanistan also had bases in northern Pakistan. They were being funded by the United States, China and Arab states, which had lined up to fight the Cold War against the Soviets. Known romantically as "freedom fighters," the mujahideen were seen as the men to rout the hated Soviets—and they understood that the way to an Afghan heart was to promise a return to their spiritual roots. But factions developed among the mujahideen. To gain popular support, each group used religion and culture to prove they were more anti-Soviet than the other. The presence of the mujahideen was very much felt in refugee centers such as Quetta, because their training camps were located in northern Pakistan. Consequently, the refugees' lives became as threatened as their compatriots' back in Afghanistan.

One of the factions, called the Taliban, which means students of Islam, seemed particularly menacing. It was made up of young men, mostly in their twenties and mostly illiterate, who had never known anything but war. They had been recruited by the increasingly militant mullahs in northern Pakistan and sent to "madrassa" schools—religious schools where, ostensibly, they studied the Koran but in fact learned to recite messages of hate. They congregated in Peshawar, in eastern Pakistan, and in Quetta, the capital of Balochistan province, which was rife with militant fundamentalists and home to Sima Samar and her son, Ali.

Although Balochistan has been officially in Pakistan since 1947, when Pakistan was created, the Durand Line, drawn between Pakistan and Afghanistan, has never been accepted by the inhabitants of the province. Consequently, the tribes of Balochistan still straddle that border and reach toward Kandahar, the Afghan city that had become home to the new and rapidly growing Taliban movement. Trouble was brewing. Sima knew it as well as she knew her work against the fundamentalists had to continue.

While the new danger lurked, she continued her anti-Soviet work with RAWA, the women's group. As long as they were resisting the Soviets, they stayed out of the gaze of the mujahideen. But the danger of their work, even here in Quetta, was brutally emphasized when their leader, Meena, was assassinated in 1987. Sima agreed to become president of RAWA and she served in that position until 1989. But during that period, she realized that the mujahideen posed as big a threat to women and girls as the Soviets had.

She watched these disturbing influences and at the same time saw how the international community's attention span waned as the Soviet regime began to weaken. When it collapsed in 1989, aid from the international community disappeared. Sima was perplexed by the sudden exodus. "Afghan refugees were no longer of interest to them. The Soviets were gone, the Cold War was over, and we were left on our own." It was a move she knew would have enormous consequences. "How could you abandon people you'd promised to help? Couldn't they see the vacuum they left would be filled by fundamentalists? They knew of the buildup of terrorism in the region. They knew human-rights laws were being abused. What did they think would happen to this area?"

While the mujahideen fought each other for power, a flood of new refugees poured into Quetta. Sima's schools and clinic were crammed with women and children who needed everything from bread and medicine to schoolbooks—and the milk of human kindness. They'd come to the right place. Despite the lack of funds and materials, she struggled to serve the people. But her struggles were confounded by the oblique threats of the newly powerful, black-turbanned Taliban, who made their presence felt throughout the refugee camps.

Meanwhile, her own house was filling with family members who'd decided Afghanistan was no longer safe. The men in her family—the father and brothers who had accused her of dishonoring their family by insisting on going to school, by refusing to marry, by taking her medical bag into rural Afghanistan to treat women and girls—now needed shelter from someone strong enough to stand up to the warriors who singled out the Hazaras for persecution. She had a houseful— her own mother, her father's second wife, all the siblings and half brothers and sisters except for the ones who had left for America. And of course her patrician papa. The people she had tried to escape from were now dependent on her, their audacious daughter and sister, for their very survival.

Sima also had a new and heart-warming addition to her family. As a student working in the resistance movement in Kabul, she and her husband had been friends with Rauf Akbeari, a clever and likeable man two years her senior. Rauf had married and become a father of a daughter, Tamanna. They had also found refuge in Quetta, but Rauf's wife had left the marriage and left Tamanna with Rauf. Sima was delighted with the smart young Tamanna, but worried that the girl's life without a mother was doomed. She would be raised by relatives, kept behind purdah walls and denied an education. As much as women were powerless, the men, in this case Tamanna's father, Rauf, were also powerless to interfere with the custom of raising a motherless child. Sima suggested he give the girl to her and that she raise Tamanna as her own child. Rauf liked the plan, and together they made it happen.

Rather than being credited with saving the future of this little girl, Sima found herself embroiled in another delicate and, as it turned out, life-threatening controversy. Her father and older brothers announced that she would marry Rauf. Sima refused, pointing out that they were guests in her house and that she was feeding and housing them. Times were changing and they should mind their own business. They had another response: she would marry Rauf or they would kill her. It was a matter of honor. A woman could not be alone. For a single mother to be raising a child was totally unacceptable to the conservative, patriarchal clan she belonged to. But Sima thumbed her nose at the family as she'd thumbed her nose at the fundamentalists. Rauf was her friend. They understood each other and worked together to make Shuhada the best non-government organization in the region. Rauf was an organizational wizard. He was also the calm in Sima's storm. Together they made a great team, but she wouldn't marry him. She provided the education, care, and protection of Tamanna and Ali with her usual tenacity. Seven years later, however, she did marry Rauf.

Trouble was brewing not only in her family home but also in Afghanistan and in Quetta. The Taliban, who had emerged victorious in Kandahar in 1994, were poised to take over the country. The tension among the displaced Afghans in the diaspora was ratcheted up again. Whisper campaigns began, gossip took on hard currency. The power struggles erupting in Afghanistan were being fueled in Quetta.

While the struggles swirled around the streets outside Sima's clinic, she was too busy trying to find funds for her hospitals and schools to get involved in what she saw as the "petty power playing of the men." Two years later, the Taliban rolled into Kabul and began one of the most misogynist regimes history had ever recorded. A new wave of refugees crowded into Quetta. She plucked the teachers and principals, the lab technicians and doctors, the logisticians and nurses from the arrivals and put them to work.

The death threats to Samar became as common as the viruses she was treating in the clinic. In what was now recognized as vintage Samar style, she told the Taliban, "You know where I am. I won't stop what I'm doing." She also developed strategies for getting around the increasingly paralyzing rules of the extremists, as well as the age-old customs of an uneducated people who believed fervently in the teachings of equally uneducated mullahs. Samar says much of the suffering of women and girls results from the mullahs' misinterpretations of the Koran, particularly those passages that focus on a woman's purity. Girls are married off as prepubescent teenagers to prevent the disastrous consequences of shaming the family honor by having relationships with boys. They're denied participation in civil society for the same reason. The rules adopted in places like Pakistan and Afghanistan put the onus on girls to prove their virginity, and excuse boys for their improprieties.

Sima took them all on and devised ingenious means to protect her patients. One day when the clinic was quiet, she suggested we drive out into the countryside. There, at the edge of what remains of a lake in this drought-stricken region, she told me about her "illegals"—and she shook her head in astonishment at her own audacity. "Let me tell you a story," she began. "A sixteen-year-old girl came with her parents to my clinic. A quick urine test and cursory examination told me what I suspected. She was six months pregnant and terrified. She had been raped. The law, according to the extremists, is that a woman who is raped must have four male witnesses to prove that she didn't cause the rape. Naturally, no such witnesses are ever available. Without them, the family is obliged to kill the girl to protect the family honor. This girl had kept her terrible secret until she could hide it no longer. I had to decide what to do. I don't approve of abortions unless there is absolutely no other way. But if I didn't do something for this girl, she would be killed. I chose life. Remember, most people here don't have any education, so I can get away with saying things they may not question. I told them their daughter had a tumor and needed surgery. I said she was too sick to have [the operation] now and she would have to stay at my clinic. I kept that girl for three months. When the baby was due, I did a cesarean section. The family waited outside the operating room because it is the custom here to show them what was found in the surgery. I put the placenta in the surgical basin, showed the so-called tumor to them and told them their daughter would be fine. Then I gave the baby to a woman who was also in trouble because she is married and infertile."

Outside Samar's clinic, troubled refugees as well as the Taliban wait in line to enter the examination rooms. Her

patients, who pay about 30 rupees ($1) per visit, come with
their full wombs and fears of infertility. They suffer all the ills
that plague refugee camps: malnutrition, anemia, typhoid fever,
malaria. In the line-ups at the door, they whisper news of the
latest atrocities and decrees of the Taliban. Today, there's a
terrible message from Jalalabad, a city in the eastern area of
Afghanistan. Yesterday, a woman tried to leave. She was
wearing her burqa but walking with a man who was not her
relative. She was arrested by the Taliban and stoned to death.
The man she was with was sentenced to seven years in prison.
There's still a hush in the clinic, when suddenly the curtain is
pushed aside and a woman appears with her Taliban husband.
They've traveled several days to get treatment at this clinic. The
Taliban know Samar is an excellent physician. (In the years to
come, they would play a cat-and-mouse game with Dr. Samar.
They knew, very well, that her clinics and schools were operating. They usually tolerated them, but shut them down when
they needed to put on a show of force. But like the Talib man
in the clinic this day, many brought their families to Samar,
even while their superiors threatened to kill her.) The Talib tells
Samar his wife bleeds from her nose whenever she works hard
in the fields. Samar raises her voice, "She's full-term pregnant,
she shouldn't be working so hard." The man replies, "She has
to work. Fix her nose."

Another young woman has been menstruating for eleven
months. Her blood pressure is dangerously low. She's as weak
as a sparrow. Except for the dark circles under her eyes, her
face is the color of bread dough. The doctor says she needs a
D&C (dilatation and curettage), but culture interferes again.
She's a virgin. The simple operation would destroy her virginity, which in turn would destroy her life. So, abdominal surgery
is scheduled. Sima admits the girl to the hospital, a former residence she has converted, with wards for men and wards for
women on one side of the courtyard, an examination room and

pharmacy on the other side, and an operating room joining the
two wings of the building. Interestingly, her operating room
has the lowest infection rate in Balochistan. As the girl's family
prepares to leave, Samar reminds them she needs a blood donor
for the surgery and calls after them, "Go get me blood from
your family and don't bring me anyone who's been fooling
around sexually or taking opium." The family members scurry
away to find the donor.

The next morning, after a cousin has been procured and the
blood has been drawn and bagged for the surgery, two doctors,
one assistant and three nurses scrub and gather in the operating room and the surgery begins. A tumor the size of a twelve-
week fetus—a large baked potato—is removed. Samar doesn't
think it's malignant but needs to send it to the laboratory to be
sure. Nor does she think it will re-grow. But it's not her call.
As custom requires, she must show the family what she found
and have them decide. She sends a nurse to the door of the
operating room that opens to the courtyard outside, where
the girl's family hover to discuss the results. They must decide
whether the girl should have a hysterectomy or not. After much
discussion, they decide on the hysterectomy. Samar doesn't
like their decision and tells the nurse to "go back out there
and talk to them. She is unmarried. No one will marry her if
she has a hysterectomy. Ask the family to give her a chance,
we can maybe save this uterus." Eventually, Samar goes
outside herself. She's holding the fibroid tumor in a basin.
There's high drama as the father, mother, sisters and aunts
question Dr. Samar. A hospital worker is dispatched on foot
to the lab in town, but it will take ten days to get the results.
At last Samar wins the debate. She returns to the operating
room, sews the girl up and makes a bet with her staff that the
results will be fine. And she says, "At least this surgery couldn't
have been done with a D&C. The girl would have required
abdominal surgery anyway."

As the war against women continued, a new and menacing problem started to turn up at the clinic. "Almost every women I see has osteomalacia," she said. "Their bones are softening due to a lack of vitamin D, which comes from sunshine. They survive on a diet of tea and naan because they can't afford eggs and milk, and to complicate matters, their burqas and veils deprive them of the sunshine. On top of that depression is endemic here because the future is so dark."

Samar was angry with what she saw as all talk and no action on the part of world organizations that claimed to be pressing ahead with issues for women. "The UN held a meeting in Quetta in early 1997 for all the various factions to discuss Afghanistan," she says. "They met at a hotel for three days. Can you imagine what that cost? And the meeting was for men only. The women were invited to meet for one hour on a different day." There's more. She was invited by Senator Harold Brown to attend a meeting in Washington a few weeks later, also to discuss the situation in Afghanistan. Each delegate was allowed six minutes to speak. Samar was the only woman. She told the gathering, "I represent more than half the people in Afghanistan. How come I only get the same six minutes as all these men?"

In the meantime, the line-up at Dr. Samar's clinic grew longer every year. Her schools for girls had to work in shifts because she didn't have the money to rent more space. The women in the cities mounting the resistance movement became discouraged in the face of the silence from the world community. And some international agencies began to cave in to the classic apologia of abusive regimes by saying, "At least there's peace under the Taliban." For the women, living in prison isn't peace. The threat of being stoned to death isn't peace. Painting your windows over so you can't be seen isn't peace. Being without music isn't peace. And so they waited, for peace.

They waited five long years while their cities and villages fell into disrepair, and their hopes and dreams crumbled along with the lives they had left behind. Dr. Samar traveled to Germany, the United States and Canada, begging people to listen to her story about the women of Afghanistan and seeking funds to support them. In what now looks like an overnight success story—which has taken up most of her forty-seven years—Sima Samar has gone from mounting the charge to unseat the leaders to leading the battle as one of them. It is surely the biggest challenge she has ever faced. "It's a six-month appointment," she said when the announcement was made in December 2001. "I'll do the best I can." All that means is giving birth to a new Afghanistan while guarding its long and extraordinary history. It's a good thing it's not the first miracle she's been asked to perform.

Chapter 3

OUT OF THE ASHES

There's a story about Afghanistan that pundits and historians tell to define the country's attitude toward foreigners. It goes like this: In 1842, during the first Anglo-Afghan war, a bloodied Englishman rode his exhausted horse into a British stronghold in Jalalabad, Afghanistan. Sir William Brydon was the only English survivor of 16,000 crack British soldiers and more than 12,000 dependents, including women and children, in a fierce battle against Afghans, while the convoy sought safe passage to India. For days afterwards, bonfires burned at the gate of the fort and bugles sounded to guide any other survivors to safety. But none ever came. It was a massacre

British colonists never forgot, and the bloodiest defeat Britain had ever known—all at the hands of local tribesmen who used their canny sense of their challenging land and a hand-hewn collection of weapons to rid their country of foreign occupiers.

The message: Don't mess with Afghanistan. They've been invaded, conquered, burned out, looted, and left as history's debris for 5,000 years. But outsiders have never been able to tame this land or its diverse people. Not the Persian King Darius I, not Alexander the Great, not the formidable Genghis Khan, not the British nor the Russians—and certainly not the medieval theocracy called the Taliban.

Through the millenia, the history of Afghanistan has chronicled a series of pyrrhic victories, won at as great a cost to the victor as the vanquished. The rogues, raiders, charlatans, and kings who ruled—or tried to rule—this daunting land enacted a story of brutal invasions, killing fields and savage revenge. It is also a story of a diverse, complicated, fascinating people who share two traits: they are passionately devoted to their turf and their culture, and they refuse to be ruled by outsiders.

Afghanistan, a country of 652,000 square kilometers (252,000 square miles)—of which less than 10 percent is arable—is about the size of Canada's province of Manitoba or America's state of Texas. The population today is estimated at between 17.7 and 23.7 million, with more than 2.5 million refugees living in Pakistan and Iran.

Centuries of invading warriors have left their mark, making Afghans a people as varied as their regions. The five major tribes have warred with each other endlessly. The Tajiks live in the northwest around Herat, the nomadic Turkmen and Uzbeks live in the central part of the north. The Hazaras, whose origins are traced back to the Mongolian rulers, live in the central mountain region. In the south and southwest are the majority tribe, the Pashtun. Among them, they speak thirty-two languages, the official ones today being Dari (Persian) and

Pashto. The unifying factor, if there is one, is that almost all Afghans are Muslim, 85 to 90 percent Sunni, the rest Shi'ite.

The culture is a rich tapestry of crafts, food and music. The hand-woven Afghan rugs, the cucumber and yogurt salads, the marinated lamb kabobs and the sound of music from the rubab, a three-stringed deeply resonant lute, are as much a part of Afghanistan as are the fat-tailed sheep and the Persian lambs that graze anywhere a patch of grass is available.

Sheep are the staple of agriculture, providing meat and fat for food as well as skins and wool for clothing. Persian lamb (or Karakul) with its dark, curly fleece used for fur, is a major Afghan export. Fine horses are the pride of many tribesmen. While there is mineral wealth and deposits of coal, copper and sulfur in the north, it's the oil deposits along the northern border that are attracting attention today. Geologists estimate about fifty billion barrels, by far the biggest untapped reserves in the world; Saudi Arabia, the world's largest oil producer, has about thirty billion barrels remaining. Reaching the deposits, however, poses an immense problem: of the 18,000 kilometers (11,000 miles) of existing roads, less than 20 percent are paved, and in 1999 the railway had only about twenty-five kilometers (15 miles) functioning.

Afghanistan is bordered by Iran on the west, Pakistan on the south and east, and by Turkmenistan, Uzbekistan and Tajikistan on the north. A finger of land reaching China and Kashmir on the northeast is the area Marco Polo called the "roof of the world."

There are five major cities. Kabul, the capital, is in the mountainous central region. In the northwest, near Iran, Herat, long known as the "key to India" by the British, is one of the oldest centers of civilization. Mazar-e-Sharif, in the north, is the home of the famous Blue Mosque. Legend says that Caliph Ali, cousin and son-in-law of the Prophet Muhammad and leader of the Shi'ite division of Islam, was killed and buried there. Jalalabad, east of Kabul, leads to the Khyber Pass and south to Peshawar in Pakistan. This was the route used by invaders from prehistoric days. And Kandahar, in the southwest, is a beautiful city that gained sudden notoriety when it became known as the spiritual home of the Taliban.

An awesomely beautiful country with a rich mix of people and places that still reflects a rugged romanticism, its landscape offers a palette of artists' colors. Ocher, copper, green and gold hues spill off the towering Hindu Kush, with its immense mountain ranges and peaks of 7,300 metres (24,000 feet) and its death-defying mountain passes fanning out to the steppes below. Beige deserts mix with lush green forests and velvety brown mountains. Snow-capped peaks contrast with the pink sandstone cliffs around Bamian, where colossal Buddhist statues were carved 1,500 years ago. They stood as an emblem of ancient civilization until the Taliban dynamited them into oblivion in March 2001. Fertile valleys fall between the unforgiving desert climes in the south and southwest and the mountain ranges that divide the country north and south. The temperatures are extreme, ranging from the temperate Kandahar to the harsh winter climes of the regions spilling out of the Hindu Kush. The fertile valleys make Afghanistan known for its almond groves, the famous peaches and grapes of Kandahar, and the castor beans that grow in the north. The highlands in the north have the finest lapis lazuli in the world. The rivers are wild and most are unnavigable, but two are the source of hydroelectric power—the Helmand, which flows southwest from the Hindu Kush to the Iranian border, and the Kabul River, which flows through the capital city and into the famous Khyber Pass, with its ninety-two bridges and thirty-four tunnels along its forty-kilometer (twenty-five-mile) route.

Before the discovery of sea routes to the Far East, Afghanistan was on the main thoroughfare, the Silk Road, which carried traders and missionaries between the Mideast and the Far East for the riches and rewards they sought. The ancient byways come together at the crossroads between central and southern Asia and between Iran and the Arabian Sea, making Afghanistan a coveted territory—as much for today's titans of industry as it was for invaders during antiquity.

While Afghanistan's strategic location has enticed invaders throughout the centuries, its high mountain barriers have also protected the invaded. The very topography that kept Afghanistan disunited served, at the same time, to make its tribes independent and notoriously difficult to govern. Darius I annexed most of the area now known as Afghanistan to the Persian Empire between 522 and 486 B.C.E. But like almost every ruler who came after him, Darius was plagued by continual, bitter and bloody tribal revolts.

Alexander the Great conquered Persia and took the prize that was Afghanistan in 329 B.C.E., but he too could never subdue the people; constant revolts plagued his reign. He made Bactria (in northern Afghanistan with its capital at Balkh) his headquarters, which flourished for a century but then fell to conquering Parthians and other rebellious tribes.

Fighting to defend the turf is as old as the country itself, and so are parts of the culture that women struggle with even today. Honor-killing, for example, is recorded as early as the fourth century C.E., in the story of Afghan poet Rabia Balkhai. Her story and her poetry are still apotheosized by students, and particularly women. Her so-called crime of honor was falling in love with Baktash, a slave. Her father, King Kaab Ghezdari, warned her that her love for the slave was forbidden, that she could never marry a man her parents hadn't chosen. But Rabia ignored his threats. She wrote of her love for Baktash, and her volumes of poetry have earned her the title of the first Persian poet. She paid for her love with her life. Her brother killed her with a Khanjer (a huge knife). She is buried at an ancient blue mosque tucked into a beautiful mountain range with snow-capped peaks, near the city of Mazar-e-Sharif.

For centuries Afghanistan remained divided as petty rulers rose and fell, struggling against foreign conquerors. During that time, Buddhism spread from the East, but it was wiped out in 400 C.E. with the invasion of the Huns, who destroyed the Buddhist culture and left most of Afghanistan in ruins.

Although Zoroastrianism, the monotheistic religion of the Persian Empire, was started in Afghanistan about 600 B.C.E., it wasn't adopted broadly by the tribes either. The first stable religion to come to the country was Islam, which was brought by the Arabs in 652 C.E. The conquest by the Muslims in the seventh century C.E. began in what is currently west Afghanistan. From the time it was introduced, soon after the Prophet died, it took less than a hundred years to convert the entire region. By the turn of the first millennium, Afghanistan had become the center of Islamic power and civilization. In the next two centuries, the land would change hands many times. The conquering hordes from Ghor (now part of Afghanistan) would establish control in 1152, as would the brutal Genghis Khan, who invaded in 1219. His wars were marked by ruthless carnage: he burned cities and destroyed the irrigation systems of Afghanistan, turning fertile soil into permanent deserts. Although said to be a brilliant ruler and military leader, even Genghis Khan failed to uproot Islamic civilization. In fact, within two generations of his death, his heirs had become Muslim.

It was at this time that Marco Polo, the Venetian traveler, took his place in Afghan history. In 1296 and during two years of imprisonment following his journey, he wrote an account of his travels through Asia. He wrote of paper currency and asbestos, coal and other phenomena virtually unknown in Europe at the time. He wrote of tribal people selling pickled monkeys passed off as pygmies. He described sumptuous spices, sugar, curious drugs, flavorful incense, and an animal "which had hair like a water buffalo and feet like those of an elephant—an ugly beast to behold." Even Christopher Columbus consulted his copy of Marco Polo's adventures two hundred years later, when he was embarking on the voyage that would lead to his discovery of America. Although Polo's credibility has been questioned, during the Renaissance the book he wrote was the chief and almost sole Western source of information on the East. And until the late nineteenth century, there was no other European material about many parts of central Asia, making Marco Polo's records of great value to historians. On his deathbed in 1324, he said, "I didn't tell half of what I saw, because no one would have believed me."

In the meantime, small Muslim kingdoms were being founded all over Afghanistan. The Moghol Empire was established in the sixteenth century, but like the other leaders who had gone before, the Moghols couldn't rule the tribal people and were ultimately defeated by the Pashtuns. There were two factions of Pashtuns, the Ghilzai and the Abdali, who formed the Durrani dynasty but fought each other for power.

In 1708 Mir Wais, a chief of the Hotaki tribe and one of the Ghilzais, made a move to establish independence for Afghanistan. And his daughter Zainab Hotaki made a debut in the history books for the women of Afghanistan. Zainab, who is said to have been educated at home, turned into a scholar of some repute. She taught the women in her father's harem to read and write in both Pashto and Dari. She was often asked for her opinion on social and public affairs, and when Mir Wais was defeated, she went with her brothers to the negotiating table of Nadir Shah, who had come from Persia to rule over Afghanistan.

This brief mention of women in the annals of Afghan history is unusual, but then women as spokespersons and negotiators were almost unheard of in the rest of the world as well. Apart from the 1405 book called *Le Livre de la Cité des Dames,* by Christine de Pizan, which was the first to call for human rights for women (the right to education and to live and work independently), it wasn't until Olympe de Gouge presented her Rights of Women and Female Citizens to Queen Marie Antoinette in France in 1790—and Mary Wollstonecraft wrote the *Vindication of the Rights of Women* two years later in England—that women were mentioned in any other rights discourse. So, despite Afghanistan's poor record of human rights for women in the recent past, there is evidence to suggest the women of Afghanistan were in the same struggle as other women during the eighteenth century.

Conquests under Nadir Shah marked the beginning of a unified Afghanistan; after his death in 1747, his lieutenant Ahmed Shah Durrani established a state that included most of present-day Afghanistan. Durrani liberated Kandahar, defeated the Moghols, took Herat away from the Persians, and extended the Muslim Empire from Kashmir to the Arabian Sea.

His dynasty, the Durrani, gave the Afghans the name "Durrani," which they themselves frequently used. The Durrani line ended when Dost Mohammed gained power in 1826. His rule saw the emergence of a problem that would plague Afghanistan for another century. The struggle between Great Britain and Russia for control of Central Asia—as well as the British desire to guard India—led to the infamous Afghan wars. Those wars were dubbed "The Great Game" by Rudyard Kipling in his 1901 novel *Kim.* The novel tells the story of the young orphan hero, Kimball O'Hara, and his successful efforts to resist the Russian attack on India.

The first of three wars began in 1838, and though British soldiers took the major cities of the east and south, the war culminated in a massacre of the British in Kabul in 1842, when that lone British survivor rode into Jalalabad on his stumbling pony. The following decade brought the struggles that made the Khyber Pass a famous name in British military annals. Although they paid local tribesmen to guard it, the British had to patrol its rugged terrain and hazardous passages constantly or risk losing it as an escape route. The British tried to manage the many internal family disputes and tribal strife, while Russia attacked from the north. But once again, Afghan warlords and tribal chiefs defeated the better equipped, modern warriors. They traded puppet kings and local leaders until eventually the British retreated and Russia established a fixed boundary and promised to respect Afghanistan's territorial integrity. But war broke out again in 1878 between England and Afghanistan.

During that war a woman who would forever be remembered by Afghans came on the scene. Her name was Malalay. The story is told that in July 1880 she picked up the Afghan flag from the failing hands of the soldiers who'd been shot by the British and valiantly carried it forward. Her show of courage made her a hero to the Afghan people, who ultimately renamed the first school for girls and a hospital for women after her. This school would become a fountainhead for Afghan girls who would go on to establish rights for women and play leading roles in all levels of society. Malalay's efforts became a symbol of the brave struggle for recognition that Afghan women would fight for the next dozen decades.

The upshot of the war was the ousting, in 1880, of ruler Shere Ali and the establishment of Abdu Rahman Khan as Emir, until his death in 1901. In the German book *Frauen in Afghanistan* (published in 1977 in German and updated in 1985 by Nancy Hatch Dupree) author Fahima Rahimi writes that Rahman laid down more rules than anyone had in previous years, many of them affecting the status of women. Rahman clung insistently to the notion that men had to have strict control of their women and that women must be secluded in their homes unless they had permission to go outside. He abhorred adultery and called for the death penalty for those caught in the act. He said, "The honor of the people of Afghanistan consists in the honor of their women." During one British battle, he apparently told his men, "If these foreigners overrun the country, the men of Afghanistan would lose control over their wives, for according to their laws, women enjoy liberty and under them, no husband has any control over his wife."

However Emir Rahman also made changes that benefited women. He changed customary laws that in his opinion were unfair to women and claimed publicly that women were due just treatment. For example, parents could and did betroth young girls as infants. The Emir ruled that, on attaining puberty, a girl should be allowed to repudiate such arranged marriages. He also tried to change the law that required widows to be remarried to the brothers or near relatives of their deceased husbands. In 1883 Rahman declared that widows should be free to remarry whomever they wished. Laws of inheritance and personal property were also laid down in strict conformity with Islamic principles. Although some of the edicts, such as the payment of blood money, had a curious agenda. Rahman equalized the payment of blood money at 7,000 rupees for each victim. Before that, the murder of a woman cost 12 rupees and the murder of a man cost 50 rupees!

Apparently the Emir was much influenced by his wife Bobo Jan, who is featured in Rahini's book. Vivacious and stylish, she traveled widely, dressed in European fashion and went without a veil. She was an excellent horsewoman and rode with two hundred mounted female guards, each armed with a saber and carbine. She was the daughter of Amir Dost Mohammad and apparently learned her love of politics from him and then shared her expertise with her husband. It was presumably so valuable she was once sent to Mazar-e-Sharif to attempt a reconciliation with a rebellious cousin. Although women had few rights, some of them were frequently sent on missions to quell disturbances between contending parties during both the eighteenth and nineteenth centuries.

Rahman did much to institute order in his unruly land. The boundary between the then Northwest Frontier Province and Pakistan (then India) was established in 1893 and named the Durand Line for Sir Mortimer Durand. It fixed the borders of Afghanistan with British India, but it split Afghan tribal areas—leaving some tribes in what is now Pakistan. The exact status of those tribal lands was left unclear, and troubles with border tribes continue to this day. Many of these clans provided a base for the Taliban to start their march on Kabul. In 1895 the northern border with Russia was fixed again, and in 1907 both Russia and Britain signed a convention at St. Petersburg in which Afghanistan was declared outside their sphere of influence.

The Anglo-Russian agreement guaranteed the independence of Afghanistan but accepted that a British influence would remain. However, that influence was resented, especially in the First World War, when the Afghans declared neutrality but sympathized with the Muslim Turks. That feeling led to the third Anglo-Afghan war, which erupted in 1921. The Emir Amanullah quickly negotiated the Treaty of Rawalpindi with the British and then devoted himself to an earnest effort to modernize his country. He initiated a series of ambitious efforts at social and political modernization, and changed his title from Emir to King—and the country from an Emirate to a Kingdom.

Amanullah introduced radical reforms. Diplomatic and commercial relations with European and Asian states were established. The first newspapers appeared and the first museum was built. He created a constitution that guaranteed the personal freedom and equal rights of all Afghans, some of which dealt with the emancipation of women. Social reforms included a new dress code, which permitted women in Kabul to go unveiled and encouraged officials to wear Western dress. Although never officially prohibited by law, purdah (screening women from contact with strangers) and the wearing of a veil were officially discouraged. Queen Soraya, who is also profiled in Rahini's book, spoke out publicly and in print, calling upon women to shed these practices and devised for herself a broad-brimmed hat with a diaphanous veil to replace the all-enveloping chadri, or burqa. The king also campaigned against the burqa, saying, "Religion does not require women to veil their hands, feet and faces or enjoin any special type of veil." It is said that at one public function, when the king uttered these words, Queen Soraya tore off her veil amidst great applause, and the other women at the gathering followed her example.

The first school for girls, called Masturat, which means covered ones, was opened in 1921, and soon after, a hospital of the same name was opened for women. By 1923 women had freedom of choice in marriage. To all intents and purposes, the emancipation of women was underway. It was at the same time that suffragettes in North America were demanding the vote, and women from the League of Nations met in Santiago, Chile, to establish women's political and civil rights.

Amanullah's sister Serajul Bamat spoke at the opening of the Masturat hospital: "Some people are laughing at us, saying that Afghan women know only how to eat and drink. But no longer! In the past not a penny was spent on women's education. Old women discourage young women by saying their mothers and grandmothers had never starved to death just because they couldn't read or write. Because of such attitudes Afghan women were deprived of education.

"Now because of the attention being paid to education by Ghazi Amanullah, much money is being spent on education.

Knowledge is not a man's monopoly. Women also deserve to be knowledgeable. We must on the one hand bring up healthy children and, on the other hand, help men in their work. We must read about famous women in this world, to know that women can achieve exactly what men can achieve."

During a gathering to celebrate the seventh anniversary of independence, Queen Soraya said, "Do not think that our nation needs only men to serve it. Women should also take their part as women did in the early years of Islam. The valuable services rendered by women are recounted throughout history, from which we learn that women were not created solely for pleasure and comfort. From their examples we learn that we must all contribute toward the development of our nation and that this cannot be done without being equipped with knowledge. So we should all attempt to acquire as much knowledge as possible, in order that we may render our services to society in the manner of the women of early Islam."

Accordingly, fifteen women from Masturat School left Kabul in 1928 to study in Turkey. Most of these girls were daughters of the ruling family, high government officials or members of the literati. One of them was the mother of Adeena Niazi, who is now the president and was the founder of the Afghan Women's Organization in Toronto, Canada. Adeena recounts her mother's experience in Turkey. "As one of the first Afghan women to be educated abroad, my mother felt very lucky. But while they were there, they discovered there had been a coup d'état, and King Amanullah was in exile. A short time later they were told to return home immediately. My mother never completed her studies." By then the Masturat School had been renamed Malalay, after the heroine who had carried the Afghan flag in battle in 1878. Some of their graduates include Shafiqa Ziaie, who was minister without portfolio in the government from 1969 to 1972; Massoma Esmati, who became one of the members of the Loya Jirga (ruling council) in 1964; and Alia Hafeez, who became a lecturer at Kabul University.

But in the 1920s the westernization Amunallah promoted had provoked the wrath of radical Muslims, who rose in 1929 to defeat him. Mohammed Nadir Shah, placed on the throne after the suppression of the revolt, continued moderate efforts to modernize Afghanistan. During his reign, his sister Ulya Janab moved the peg for women's excellence forward when she began a translation, from Urdu to Dari, of the life of Al Farooq, the caliph Omar, who was the companion of the Prophet Muhammad. Ulya Janab had been raised in British India, where she learned to speak Urdu. Sadly, she died at an early age, but her work was later completed by Najaf Ali Khan and published in 1932.

King Nadir Shah was assassinated in 1933 and succeeded by his son Mohammad Zahir Shah, who set out to strengthen the country and to build its economy. King Zahir undertook social and economic reforms, and by the 1960s Afghan life was a curious mixture of anachronism and modernity. Afghan women were seen both veiled and unveiled, and the educational system was being expanded to include women. Little did Zahir Shah know at the time that he would be called from exile in Rome to patch together a new Afghanistan, when the Taliban were defeated and the country left in ruins once again in the fall of 2001.

During the monarchy of Zahir Shah, change was, if not rapid, constant. He appointed Prince Mohammad Daoud as prime minister. The U.S. recognized Afghanistan in 1934. Da Afghanistan Bank (the State Bank of Afghanistan) was incorporated. The king decided the country would stay neutral during the Second World War. And when Britain withdrew from India and Pakistan was carved out of India and Afghan lands in 1949, his parliament denounced the Durand Treaty and refused to recognize the Durand Line.

Afghanistan was deeply interested in the partition of India and Pakistan and in 1951 protested the incorporation of the tribal lands within the Durand Line into Pakistan. The government urged the creation of an independent or autonomous state with a Pashtun majority, to be made from the Northwest Frontier Province and to be called Pashtunistan. The dispute was complicated by the fact that the nomadic Pashtun tribes seasonally crossed the Afghan-Pakistani border with flocks of sheep. Relations grew increasingly bitter between the two countries, and in 1961 the border between them was closed and Pakistan and Afghanistan came close to war. Pakistan has never yielded the territory.

During the 1960s and 1970s, particularly while Daoud was in office, women made considerable advances. Purdah was made optional. Women began to enroll in the university, which had become co-educational. Women entered the workforce and took jobs with the government. The number of girls from the provinces attending Kabul University increased every year as did the number of women attending universities abroad. By 1963 the first women graduated from the university's medical school. The same year produced the first woman graduate of the law faculty, Hakima Mustamundi, who then went on to study in Paris where she wrote her thesis, "Offences Among Children," which was serialized in Kabul's weekly newspaper. The first two woman senators were appointed in 1965. And between 1966 and 1971 fourteen women graduated in Islamic jurisprudence and were apprenticed to courts throughout Afghanistan. Women were also appointed to senior posts in government offices. Kubra Nurzai was made Minster of Health in 1965. And sports finally became permissible for women.

In the 1960s Prime Minister Daoud began to develop close ties between Afghanistan and Russia. In January 1965 the Afghan Communist Party was secretly formed, and in

September that year, the country held its first nationwide elections under a new constitution.

In July 1973, while the king was on vacation in Europe, the government and the monarchy were overthrown in a military coup headed by Daoud and the communist party—called the Peoples Democratic Party of Afghanistan (PDPA). Daoud abolished the monarchy and declared himself president of the Republic of Afghanistan. Under the new constitution of 1975, women's rights were confirmed, but fundamentalist extremists were working against Daoud and his reforms. In 1978, in another violent communist coup, Daoud was killed and Mohammad Taraki was named president. Mass arrests and torture followed, and the mujahideen movement against the communists was born.

Those events signaled the lead-up to what would ultimately attract world attention to Afghanistan. Before the advent of the Taliban regime, the country had been operating on a rickety foundation for almost two decades after the Soviet Union's invasion in December 1979. Mohammad Najibullah, an Afghan who'd been trained by the Soviets, was brought in from the USSR to run the secret police. A brutal boot-camp rule followed, which saw some of the fiercest resistance of any wars in Afghanistan. Najibullah was then made president of the new Soviet satellite state in 1986. The mujahideen, funded by the U.S. and others, refused to deal with the puppet government and started a resistance movement against the Soviets. Using U.S. weapons and training, the resistance would ultimately claim 40,000 Soviet lives and more than 350,000 Afghan lives during the ten-year occupation.

In 1989 the Soviets withdrew in defeat. In their wake, seven different factions among the victorious mujahideen jockeyed for power, each pretending to be more religious than the other, to win the support of the people. In the process, they planted the seeds for a fratricidal bloodbath. Life under the victorious mujahideen proved to be as violent as it had been under the communists and more religiously strict than the Afghan people had ever known.

An Islamic state was formed, and in 1992 Burhanuddin Rabbani was elected president. Former president Mohammad Najibullah took refuge in the UN complex, where he stayed under virtual house arrest until 1996, when the Taliban assassinated him the day they arrived in Kabul. But other mujahideen leaders such as Rashid Dostum and Gulbudin Hekmatyar continued to clash with the Rabbani government and, in the process, reduced Kabul to ruins. The conflict became a real civil war when the mujahideen turned their guns on each other. More than 50,000 people were killed despite four Pax Romana peace agreements signed in Islamabad under the auspices of the United Nations. The climate of Afghanistan had become ferocious. While the U.S. and the Soviets had spent $3 billion each on the twentieth-century's version of the Great Game, it was the Afghan people, the pawns in the power grab, who paid the biggest price.

With the Cold War ended in 1989, the U.S. and the humanitarian aid community, astonishingly, packed up and left. Like minnows, they all turned at once, leaving the feeding ground for other, presumably more fertile spaces. Afghanistan was no longer useful as a staging ground for anti-Soviet maneuvering. The U.S. and its allies did nothing to rebuild the country they'd used like a soccer field to play out their Cold War. The vacuum created an opening for the Taliban, whose origins are in southern Afghanistan. In a galvanizing incident in 1994, religious leader Mullah Mohammad Omar gathered his students (Talibs) together to pursue and kill a mujahideen leader and his men who had sexually assaulted three young women in Kandahar. The Taliban used this pursuit to make rapid advancements against the Rabbani government, and capture most of the provinces in southern Afghanistan by 1995.

While refugees had begun leaving Afghanistan when the communists arrived in 1979, the biggest exodus occurred after the Taliban took Kabul in 1996. A short time after that, Afghanistan became a pariah state. It was internationally isolated as a major narcotics exporter and a haven for terrorists. The United Nations tried to stop the country's downward spiral by slapping sanctions on the country. The U.S. regarded Afghanistan as a rogue state for harboring terrorist Osama bin Laden, who had been accused of bombing two American embassies in East Africa. And women around the world had rallied to rescue their sisters who'd been caught in a human-rights catastrophe.

The Taliban were accused of creating the most oppressive regime women have ever suffered. The human-rights violations in Afghanistan became the worst in the world, the Hazara minority being the biggest target of Taliban wrath, after women and girls. Even the devastating earthquake that struck Afghanistan in February 1998, killing more than four thousand people and leaving thousands of people homeless, couldn't compete with the wholesale destruction the Taliban wrought on the country. They turned Afghanistan into the largest opium factory in the world, producing 70 percent of the world's heroin supply, took up arms dealing and smuggling to finance their regime, and accepted the largesse of Osama bin Laden, who used the country as a terrorist training ground.

The next chapter of Afghan history is now being written. An interim government took office on December 22, 2001, with a six-month mandate to prepare the country for a transitional government that will hold elections by 2004. While invasions, wars and insurrections have defined the past, one thing about the future is certain. Islam will continue to influence the people, the culture and, likely, the government. The Taliban's opportunistic distortion of religious doctrine led to

the current debacle in Afghanistan. The interpretation of
Islam by the post-Taliban regime will likely determine the
country's future.

Chapter 4

RELIGION:
POLITICS MADE
SACRED

When it comes to religion, interpretation is everything. When it comes to politics, everything is interpretation. So when the mullahs in Kabul began to exert control, the women and girls of Afghanistan had no choice but to bow to political tyranny, which came in the guise of a message from God.

Islam, the world's fastest-growing religion, has an estimated 1.2 billion followers. Among those followers are two different sects, the Sunni and the Shi'ite, and within the sects seventy-two recognized schools of thought. The name Islam means "self-surrender to the will of God," the same message taught by all the prophets whether they were Jews, Christians or

Muslims. However, Islam does not have a priesthood, so every Muslim is free to interpret the laws, ethics, and social organization described in the Koran according to a personal understanding. The emphasis on personal interpretation of religious doctrine has often meant that Islam is "translated" into a confounding mix of piety and ferocity that is nowhere more evident than in the lives of women and girls. Are women elevated or subjugated under Islamic rule? Is the law just or merciless? Can religious leaders—sometimes mullahs who cannot read or write—lead a people forward in the twenty-first century? Does Islam need a renaissance or a reformation?

Finding the answers requires an understanding of the origins of Islam, the intentions of the Koran and the vastly different interpretations of the doctrines it contains.

Believers accept that the Creator's messages were revealed to many prophets, including Abraham, Noah, David, Isaac, Jacob, Moses and Jesus. They also believe that these messages culminated with Muhammad, the last Prophet, 1,400 years ago. During the first six hundred years of Islam—from its genesis during the short lifetime of the Prophet Muhammad between 609 and 632, and approximately 1200—the religion spread from Mecca, where he received the revelations, to the centers of civilization such as Córdoba, Cairo and Baghdad.

During that period, Muslims were a military power but also led the world in scientific inventions. They created a sophisticated legal system and made significant contributions to the field of medicine. They made enormous advances in education and had a dramatic impact on the arts and sciences. The largest number of non-Latin words in English comes from Arabic—chemistry, music and algebra for example.

Although the Crusades—a series of wars undertaken by European Christians between the eleventh and fourteenth centuries to recover the Holy Land—are discounted by Muslim scholars for the downfall of Islam, it was at about that time,

sometime after 1200, that the Islamic world began to slip from
its dominant position. By 1800 it had become forceless, disen-
franchized and colonized. Muslim countries from Indonesia to
Morocco and the central Asian states came under the control
of European colonizing powers. It would be another 150 years
before they began to gain independence.

In the ensuing years, resistance and distrust grew among the
followers of Islam for those who had usurped their land during
colonization. Dr. Mohamed Elmasry, president of the Canadian
Islamic Congress, says, "It's only in recent years that Islam has
resurfaced as a world force. Today we're about where we were
at the time of the Prophet."

The Koran is universally accepted by Muslims as the word
of Allah or God, dictated verbatim to the Prophet through the
Angel Gabriel. It is divided into 114 units, each called a Surah,
and is the principal source of Islamic law, which is known as
Shari'a. While Muslims believe the Koran is the divine truth,
they also believe the Koran contains the rules by which the
Muslim world is governed or should govern itself. The Shari'a
details the way a Muslim society is organized and governed,
and it provides the means to resolve conflicts among individuals and between the individual and the state. The other source
Muslims refer to is the Sunnah of the Hadith (Traditions of the
Prophet), which is the record of speeches of the Prophet and
accounts of his deeds recorded by his companions. The Hadith
is used to explain passages in the Koran, and Muslim scholars
claim that each passage or verse cannot be explained apart
from its context in the Hadith.

There are five pillars of faith for Muslims. The devout must
face in the direction of Mecca and pray five times a day to adhere
to the path of righteousness and resist indecency and evil. They
must pay an annual tax to support the needy and fulfill other
objectives of the community; this is to remind Muslims that all
beneficence comes from the bounty of God. They must fast

from dawn to sunset during the month of Ramadan, the ninth month of the Islamic calendar, which usually coincides with November in the Gregorian calendar. The fast involves abstaining from eating, drinking, smoking and marital intercourse, to remind believers of their dependence upon God. They should make a pilgrimage, known as Hajj, to Mecca once in their lifetime, if they have the physical and financial means to do so. The Hajj emphasizes repentance and results in forgiveness from God. It also strengthens the bond of the faithful from all walks of life and regions of the world. And they must accept Islam's creed, which begins, "There is no God but Allah, and Muhammad is his messenger." The Arabic expression "La Darar Wa La Derar," which means Do Nothing to Harm Yourself or Others, is the fundamental rule of Islam.

Muslim scholars do not consider Islam to be an evolving religion, but rather a fixed religious and legal system, as relevant to contemporary society as it was in the time of the Prophet. They claim that with disciplined interpretation and with the aid of the Hadith and other sources of interpretation, Islam can, as intended, provide the solution to contemporary social problems. The situation in Afghanistan and many other parts of the Muslim world, such as northern Nigeria and Saudi Arabia, suggests the need to examine those claims more closely.

There are hundreds (if not thousands) of Muslim scholars who interpret the Koran and analyze its 114 Surahs for modern living. One of the leading scholars is Dr. Jamal Badawi, the Egyptian author of *Gender Equity in Islam: Basic Principles,* first published in 1995 and revised in 1999. In his book, he discusses various rights for women and interprets the Koran and the Hadith and the messages that are often questioned not only by non-Muslims but by Muslims as well. Here's an abridged version of what the Koran, according to Dr. Badawi, says and does not say about women:

- Under no circumstance does the Koran encourage, allow or condone family violence or physical abuse. Although Surah 4:34 states in part, "As to those women on whose part you fear disloyalty and ill conduct, admonish them [first], [next] do not share their beds, [and last] beat [tap] them [lightly]; but if they return to obedience, seek not against them means [of annoyance]." The maximum measure is limited by the following: it must be seen as a rare exception to the repeated exhortation of mutual respect, kindness and good treatment; it is not permissible to strike anyone's face, cause any bodily harm or be harsh; it does not imply desirability.

- Both genders are entitled to equality before the law and courts of law. Justice is genderless. One common but erroneous belief is that a woman's testimony is one-half of a man's testimony. A survey of all passages in the Koran relating to testimony does not substantiate this. The issue of equality between the genders is found in the Prophet's statement, "Women are but sisters or twin halves of men."

- The Koran (2:228) states: "And they [women] have rights similar to those [of men] over them, and men have the right to revoke divorce within the specified waiting period and make peace with the divorced wife." This refers to the natural difference between the sexes, which entitles the weaker sex to protection. It implies no superiority or advantage before the law.

- There is no decree in Islam that forbids women from seeking employment. No jurist is able to point to an explicit text in the Koran that categorically excludes women from any lawful type of employment. However, Islam regards a woman's role in society as a mother and wife as her most sacred and essential one.

- Education is not only a right but a responsibility for all males and females. The Prophet Muhammad said, "Seeking knowledge is mandatory for every Muslim."

- The female has the right to accept or reject marriage proposals. Her consent is a prerequisite to the validity of the marital contract. If an arranged marriage means marrying a female without her consent, then such a marriage may be annulled if the female so wishes.
- Divorce is a last resort, permissible but not encouraged.
- The custody of young children (up to the age of about seven) is given to the mother. A child later may choose the mother or father as his or her custodian.
- The practice of polygamy was common in Biblical times. No text in the Koran explicitly specifies either monogamy or polygamy as the norm, although demographic data indicates strongly that monogamy is the norm and polygamy the exception. Islam did not outlaw polygamy, as many other people and religious communities did, but it was the only Abrahamic religion that regulated and restricted it. The only passage in the Koran (4:3) that explicitly addresses polygamy and restricts its practice in terms of the number of wives permitted—and the requirement of justice between them on the part of the husband—was revealed after the battle of Uhud, in which dozens of Muslims were martyred, leaving behind widows and orphans. This provides a moral, practical and humane solution to the problem of widows and orphans, who would otherwise surely be more vulnerable in the absence of a husband and father figure in terms of economics, companionship, proper child-rearing and other needs.
- The general rule in political and social life is participation and collaboration of males and females in public affairs.
- There is no text in the Koran that precludes women from any position of leadership, except in leading prayer; women, however, may lead other women in prayer.
- Parents are duty bound to show kindness and justice to their daughters.

- The husband is responsible for the maintenance, protection and overall leadership of the family within the framework of consultation and kindness. The mutuality and complementarity of husband and wife does not mean subservience by either party to the other.
- The laws of inheritance afford the male twice the inheritance of a female, and they afford women greater financial guarantees than men. Males inherit more but are financially responsible for their female relatives (Koran 4:7).
- Financial security is assured for women. They are entitled to receive marital gifts without limit and to keep present and future properties and income for their own security, even after marriage.
- The basic right to personal possession of property applies equally to males and females. More specifically the Shari'a (Islamic Law) recognized the full property rights of women before and after marriage.
- The key to proper dress and behavior for females and males alike is modesty. The Koran does not mention seclusion of women or covering the face in a burqa.

Islam doctrine, therefore, is protective, forgiving and respectful of women. The worldly observance of that doctrine is another matter entirely. Muslim women claim they are beaten by their husbands, with no recourse in the courts. They often lose everything, including their children, when a husband decides to walk out on the marriage. They have second-class status compared to the men in their lives.

And what about the ultra-conservative clerics, in places like Bangladesh and Pakistan, who assail women's groups as evil? An Associated Press report out of Karak, Pakistan, in July 2001, said the clerics there rail against internationally financed aid organizations and their promotion of women's and girls' education and small home businesses. They hurl curses at the women who work for these groups, calling them evil hand-maidens of a decadent West, which wants to destroy Islamic traditions. The clerics urge the faithful to shun Pakistani women involved with such groups as prostitutes or, alternatively, to kidnap them, force them into marriage and keep them locked away at home. "If you see any one of them, just take her home and forcibly marry her. If she's a foreigner, kill her," says cleric Maulana Zia-ul Haq. In the same report, another cleric, Maulana Sakhi Badshah, says, "We are trying to create hatred against these organizations. We are preaching against them in our mosques, in our gatherings, even at our funerals. They are preaching obscenity, vulgarity and Christianity." To make sure the onlookers are getting his point, Badshah shouts, "Women should stay in the home. These people say that men and women are equal. Of course they are not. Women cannot be as smart as a man."

In July 2001 a small bomb was shoved into the drainpipe of a woman's self-help group called Sisters' Home in Karak. A hand grenade was tossed into the office of another group. These kinds of actions—and skewed interpretations of the Koran—are even worse in Afghanistan. In the Afghan city of Herat, Hafisa Rashid was wearing the prescribed burqa, but she made the unforgivable error of letting her ankles show. The Taliban said she was dressed promiscuously and sentenced her to forty lashes. A member of the Taliban Ministry for the Propagation of Virtue and the Suppression of Vice publicly wielded the whip, which left long, ugly scars down her back. The wounds healed, but the scars remind her that her gender does not allow her safe passage anywhere in her country.

Dr. Badawi admits, in *Gender Equity in Islam,* "There exists a gap between the normative behavior regarding women outlined in the Koran and the prevalent reality among Muslims, both as societies in the Muslim world and as communities in the West." The differences in religious observation and lifestyles in the liberal West and the ultra-restrictive regions of the Muslim world create dichotomies that suggest the Koran can be interpreted however the local power-brokers want. Clearly, some of those interpretations have been damaging to women. Dr. Badawi sees both extremes as wrong. "Some Muslims emulate non-Islamic cultures and adopt modes of dress, unrestricted mixing, and behavior, which influence them and endanger their families' Islamic integrity and strength. On the other hand, in some Muslim cultures, undue and excessive restrictions for women, if not their total seclusion, is believed to be the ideal. Both extremes seem to contradict the normative teachings of Islam and are inconsistent with the virtuous yet participatory nature of both men and women in society at the time of the Prophet Muhammad." During the prophetic period, women were not excluded or secluded. They participated with men in acts of worship, such as prayers and pilgrimage, in learning and teaching, in the marketplace, in the discussion of public issues (political life) and in the battlefield when necessary.

Dr. Badawi says, "There are enough indications to show that a gap does exist between the ideal and the real. Given the existence of such a gap, a wide gap at times, it follows that Muslim reformers and other international bodies and movements share at least one thing in common: an awareness of the need to close or at least narrow that gap."

Although militant interpretations of Islam have thrust the religion into a blazing spotlight that makes many Muslims feel uncomfortable, it would be a travesty to depict Islam as the only religion that subordinates women. Dr. Sherif Abdel Azeem, a scholar at Cairo University in Egypt, reminds us that Western attitudes toward Islam resulted in banning girls from school who were wearing a veil—a headscarf actually—as was done in France in 1995. "A young Muslim student wearing a headscarf is denied her right to education in France—the land of Voltaire—while a Catholic student wearing a cross or a Jewish student wearing a skullcap are not." He launched a study, in 1995, of the doctrines in the three monotheistic religions. His paper, titled, "Women in Islam Versus Women in the Judaeo-Christian Tradition: The Myth and the Reality," discusses the contentious issues often raised about religious doctrine.

He points out that Christian and Jewish texts don't favor or offer more equality to women than does Islam. For example, the Catholic Bible states: "The birth of a daughter is a loss" (Ecclesiasticus 30:3; this book is also known as Sirach). And that passage continues, "A man who educates his son will be the envy of his enemy." It also says, "Keep a headstrong daughter under firm control, or she will abuse any indulgence she receives. Keep a strict watch on her shameless eye, do not be surprised if she disgraces you" (Ecclesiasticus 26: 10–11).

The attitude of St. Paul in the New Testament is even more blatantly sexist. "As in all the congregations of the saints, women should remain silent in the churches. They are not allowed to speak, but must be in submission as the law says. If they want to inquire about something, they should ask their own husbands at home: for it is disgraceful for a woman to speak in the church" (I Corinthians 14:34–35). On the other hand, the Koran says a woman has the right to argue with the Prophet. No one has the right to instruct her to be silent. She is under no obligation to consider her husband the one and only reference in matters of law and religion.

Dr. Azeem also points out that Jewish laws concerning menstruating women are extremely restrictive. "The Old Testament considers any menstruating woman as unclean and impure. Moreover her impurity infects others as well. Anyone or anything she touches becomes unclean for a day [Leviticus 15:19–23]. No wonder many women still refer to menstruation as 'the curse.'"

It is true that the Koran instructs believers dealing with financial transactions to get two male witnesses or one male and two females. However, it's also true that in other situations the Koran accepts the testimony of a woman as equal to a man's. Contrast that with the fact that, in modern Israel, women are not allowed to give any evidence in rabbinical courts—even when the case directly affects them.

Adultery is considered a sin in all religions. The Bible decrees the death sentence for both the adulterer and the adulteress (Leviticus 20:10). Islam also equally punishes the adulterer and the adulteress (Surah 24:2). However, adultery, according to the Koran, is the involvement of a married man or a married woman in an extramarital affair. The Bible only considers the extramarital affair of a married woman as adultery (Leviticus 20:10; Deuteronomy 22:22; and Proverbs 6:20–7, 7:27).

The Talmud describes the financial situation of the wife as follows: "How can a woman have anything; whatever is hers belongs to her husband. What is his is his and what is hers is also his . . . Her earnings and what she may find in the streets are also his. The household articles, even the crumbs of bread on the table are his. Should she invite a guest to her house and feed him, she would be stealing from her husband" (Sanhedrin 71a, Gittin 62a).

Until the late nineteenth and early twentieth centuries, under canon and civil law, a woman in Christian Europe and America lost her property rights upon marriage. Dr. Azeem describes a system in which a married woman was practically treated as an infant in the eyes of the law. "The wife simply belonged to her husband and therefore she lost her property, her legal personality and her family name." Until the late 1960s, most women had to promise to obey when they took their marriage vows. In Canada, a married woman couldn't open a bank account without her husband's signature until the early 1970s. Nor could she have treatment in a hospital or take her own children to the hospital for treatment without her husband's signature.

The Biblical rules of inheritance are outlined in Numbers 27: 1–11. A wife is given no share in her husband's estate. A daughter can inherit only if no male heirs exist. A mother is not an heir at all, but the father is. Widows and daughters—in the case where male children remained—were at the mercy of the male heirs for provision. That is why widows and orphan girls were among the most destitute members of Jewish society. Until late in the nineteenth century, so were mothers and daughters in Christian society. As for Muslims, Azeem says, "Mothers, wives, daughters and sisters had received inheritance rights 1,300 years before Europe recognized these rights ever existed."

Azeem highlights remarkable differences in the three religions in their attitude toward divorce. Christianity abhors divorce altogether. Jesus said, "But I tell you that anyone who divorces his wife, except for marital unfaithfulness, causes her to become an adulteress, and anyone who marries a divorced woman commits adultery" (Matthew 5:32). "This uncompromising ideal assumes a state of moral perfection that human societies have never achieved," Azeem writes. "Judaism, on the other hand, allows divorce even without a cause. The Old Testament gives the husband the right to divorce his wife even if he just dislikes her" (Deuteronomy 24:1–4). Wives, on the other hand, cannot initiate divorce under Jewish law unless they have a Get certificate before the marriage is performed. Jewish women—even in New York and Toronto—are still yoked to ancient laws that say they can't get a divorce unless they have a Get. A Get can only be given by a man. Without it, any child born of a second marriage is called a Maumzer, and Maumzers cannot marry except to another Maumzer. Islam falls between Christian and Jewish tenets: it recognizes divorce, but discourages it by all means.

The veil is another contentious issue. Westerners are perplexed by the concept of women covering themselves in public. But Jewish women were once expected to cover their heads, and today some Jewish women, those who belong to the Hasidic sects, for example, still cover their heads by wearing a wig. In Christianity, nuns covered their heads for hundreds of years, and women attending Protestant and Catholic churches were expected to wear hats until well into the 1960s. The Koran makes it clear that the veil is essential for modesty. "O Prophet, tell your wives and daughters and the believing women that they should cast their outer garments over their bodies [when abroad] so that they should be known and not molested" (Surah 33:59). Like other Muslim scholars, Azeem says this was for protection rather than oppression.

In the twenty-first century, one question needs to be asked: Do women in the Muslim world today receive this noble treatment? The answer is no. Azeem argues, "There is a wide spectrum of attitudes toward women in the Muslim world today." Nevertheless, he says, certain trends are discernible. As most scholars of Islam agree, the first problem lies in the deviation from the ideals of Islam with respect to the status of women. One side holds the views of the liberal West, the other clings to the restricted, tradition-oriented view of ultra-conservativism. "The Muslim world is in need of a renaissance that will bring it closer to the ideals of Islam and not further from them." To sum up, he says, "The notion that the poor status of Muslim women today is because of Islam is an utter misconception." He feels it is not an attachment to Islam but rather a detachment from it that has created problems for women. But, he also says, it's time to address those problems. "So many Muslim women have been denied their basic Islamic rights for so long. The mistakes of the past have to be corrected. To do that is not a favor, it is a duty incumbent upon all Muslims. The worldwide Muslim community has to issue a charter of Muslim women's rights based on the instructions of the Koran and the teachings of the Prophet of Islam."

That task is immense because the schools of thought are so varied. From Sufism—the inner, mystical, or psycho-spiritual dimension of Islam—to Wahhabism, which is the dour, repressive creed practiced in Saudi Arabia and espoused by Osama bin Laden and other Islamic fundamentalists throughout the world, the distance between spirituality and extremism is vast. Even the two major sects, the Sunnis, which comprise about 85 percent of all Muslims today, and the Shi'ite, which make up the rest, differ according to governance.

Barbara Ehrenreich, a columnist for *The Progressive,* a journalistic voice for peace and social justice, sees the Taliban's imposition of Wahhabism in Afghanistan as their presumption that Sufism needed to be stamped out.

For Ehrenreich, "Islamic fundamentalism is a response not to the West or to the modern, but to earlier strands of Islam, just as Protestantism was a response to Catholicism. Wahhabism arose in response to the [thoroughly Muslim] Ottoman Empire and to the indigenous Sufism of eighteenth-century Arabia."

She says the closest Christian counterpart to today's Islamic fundamentalists were the Calvinists. "In sixteenth-century Swiss cantons and seventeenth-century Massachusetts, Calvinists and Calvinist-leaning Protestants banned dancing, gambling, drinking, colorful clothing and sports of all kinds. They outlawed idleness and vigorously suppressed sexual activity in all but its married, reproductively oriented form." And in a twist to the current abhorrence of fundamentalism in the West, Calvinism—or Puritanism as it was known in America—was immensely successful. So, we might ask, are today's Muslim fundamentalists the Calvinists of Islam? And if they are, can women play a role in re-casting or re-interpreting its original doctrine? Since Islam, if properly interpreted, is not any more oppressive to women than Christianity or Judaism, women may very well be the ones to shift the religion back to its true doctrine.

Most mainstream Christians and Jews have pressured their religious leaders to modernize the interpretations of religious doctrines—from the Bible and the Talmud. Countries like Afghanistan and Pakistan have gone in the opposite direction. The Hudood Ordinances adopted in Pakistan in 1979 are a prime example. One needs to ask whether they offer a correct religious interpretation of the Koran or simply a government's annihilation of the human rights of girls and women.

The Hudood Ordinances were promulgated two years after a coup by Army Chief-of-Staff General Zia-ul-Haq. General Zia-ul-Haq headed a martial-law regime that embarked on a program of Islamizing Pakistan's laws and legal institutions in order to secure his legitimacy. He used religion for his own political ends.

The most far-reaching of the Hudood Ordinances are those that govern adultery, fornication, rape and prostitution (which is called *zina*), bearing false testimony *(qazf),* as well as theft and drinking alcohol. In effect, the Ordinances criminalize extramarital sex, establish separate ages of majority for men and women, and dramatically narrow the definition of rape. Not surprisingly, the promulgation of *zina* was followed by a sharp increase in the number of women and even young girls in prison.

The Ordinances define the age of majority as sixteen for females and eighteen for males—or the attainment of puberty for either. Because the Ordinances abolished Pakistan's statutory rape law, girls as young as twelve have been prosecuted for having extramarital intercourse under circumstances that would have previously seen statutory rape charges brought against the assailant. Accordingly, the threat of being charged with adultery or other sexual misconduct prevents many women from reporting rape. Attaining majority at puberty also exposes young children to the prospect of Hadd (Koranic) punishments, including whipping, amputation and death by stoning.

Women's groups in Pakistan have been fighting these Ordinances for twenty years, arguing that the power elites have fraudulently interpreted the Koran for political gain. For example, although the Koran says a woman's testimony is admissible (except for issues involving financial transactions), under the Hudood Ordinances the testimony of women is not admissible, nor is the testimony of a non-Muslim. So if a Muslim man rapes a Muslim woman, he cannot be convicted— simply because she cannot testify against him. Moreover, marital rape is not a crime. An estimated 80 percent of women in Pakistan are victims of domestic violence, yet the police rarely investigate—and police corruption and violence go unpunished. Even in cases where the woman dies of burns apparently caused during cooking, the police usually do not investigate, because they assume the woman has been killed for infidelity. When women do escape the violence, the police usually return them to their abusive husbands. The Human Rights Commission of Pakistan reported that more than a thousand women died in Pakistan in 1999 as victims of honor-killing, which was generally committed by their husbands or brothers.

Male violence against women has no legal sanction. Moreover, although 95 percent of the women accused of prosti-tution (*zina*) are found innocent, either in court or on appeal, the women charged still have to face the stigma of being accused and are often subjected to sexual abuse while detained. While the Hudood Ordinances seek to define and reinforce the notion of a pure and chaste Pakistani citizen, the reality is quite different.

The apparent war against women—in the form of the Hudood Ordinances—is as confounding for Muslim scholars as is the interpretation of terms such as Jihad (holy war), Hijab (Islamic dress) and martyrdom, thus altering the intent of some passages of the Koran.

Jihad is a notion that has been wrongfully appropriated by political opportunists who seek power and revenge. Many have come to associate Jihad with the massacre of innocents. In fact, the Koran refers to Jihad as advancing peace and justice. Taken from the Arabic root Ga-Ha-Da, it means exerting an effort, expounding an energy, striving, working to improve, struggling, doing one's best. According to the Surahs, Jihad is the stand taken for those who are oppressed or forced out of their homes because of their religion (Surah 22:39–40).

Launching Jihad requires knowledge, effort, resources, activism, awareness, praying, persuasion, combativeness and advocacy (Surah 8:60, 9:44–45, 9:111). And military force is used if it is the only option to stop a greater evil (Surah 2:216). Jihad is not meant to achieve personal, territorial or economical gains and not to exercise power and control (Surah 2:190–191). Nor can there be Jihad for those who are after personal, tribal and national gains (Surah 9:24).

So how did Jihad get tied to terrorism? How has it become a buzzword for violence? It is often translated into English not only as "a holy war," but also a war waged against non-Muslims, a kind of reverse Crusade.

Dr. Elmasry is angry with the militant use of Jihad and what he sees as a self-serving slant on Islam. "Using religion to justify violence is wrong because that affects 1.2 billion people around the world. They take my faith and use it for violence. [The Christian fundamentalists who are] killing doctors who perform abortions and frightening others who are non-Christian, by saying they will go to hell and using 'Jesus as Savior' to justify it, are also wrong. What the [terrorist] pilots did in America was not Jihad. It was [inventing] a sacred excuse for murder."

But he admits that some Muslims must bear responsibility for the bad name given to Jihad. "Today some contemporary governments and groups in Muslim countries make reference to Jihad only in its military meaning, through words and deeds, in order to hide their moral, social and political bankruptcy. In the process, they kill the innocent, cause only death and destruction, and do not advance the cause of peace and justice. Regrettably, they are the ones who show up regularly in the newspapers and on television."

As for Hijab (Islamic dress) most Muslim scholars agree the Koran calls for conservative dress, not the concealment of a woman's face. And most feminist scholars say that as long as a woman makes the decision for herself, rather than being forced by male power elites into seclusion, the wearing of Hijab is a personal choice.

Martyrdom is another thorny issue. Soon after September 11, a story circulated that said Muslims who sacrifice their lives for Allah will find seventy-two young virgins waiting for them in paradise, making suicide religiously correct in Islam. I asked Dr. Elmasry if this story had more to do with politics made sacred than religious doctrine made manifest. He said, "The interpretation that refers to seventy-two virgins comes from an obscure book written by an ancient scholar using his own opinion of the wording in the Koran. As for suicide, the Koran is categorically opposed to this."

Once again, interpretation confounds the supposed "true" meaning of the Koran. The problems invariably lie in the transliteration of words, some as simple as replacing the word "friend" with the word "overlord." For example, a rabbi interpreted a passage in the Koran this way: "Take not Christians and Jews for friends. If you do, you are one of them." And a Muslim interpreted the same passage as saying,

"Take not Christians and Jews as overlords; they will control you."

The conundrum behind these differing interpretations is that Islamic doctrine suggests that every Muslim is free to interpret religion according to his (or, on rare occasions, her) own understanding. There isn't one voice or one collection of voices that speaks for all Muslims. In fact, the scholars who do speak out claim their views are rarely carried in the Western press and their often-vociferous denunciations of the militants go unreported. When the Taliban destroyed the two giant 1,500-year-old Buddhist stone statues in Afghanistan in March 2001, most Muslims saw the act as a perversion of the Koran. A delegation of scholars led by Youssef Alqaradawi, dean of Islamic Studies at Qatar University, met with the Taliban shortly after the statues had been destroyed. They told the Taliban that Islam forbids insulting the God of another religion and that this action would do harm to Muslims and compromise their safety in Buddhist countries such as Japan and China. They also warned the Taliban that the action would pit the international community against them. The Taliban's response was a denunciation of the international community and its fuss over the statues when Afghanistan had so many other problems the rest of the world had ignored. They also accused the delegation of ignoring their problems and only turning up because of the condemnation surrounding the destruction of the statues. The Taliban's explanation for destroying the cultural icons was that the Prophet had destroyed statues on his way to Mecca.

Like many other sects within Islam, the Taliban only have basic knowledge of the Koran. For the most part, members have had no formal education. They'd been taught by mullahs who weren't educated, hadn't studied the Koran, and made things up as they went along. They were never exposed to the outside world and never held jobs outside of soldiering. Their initial goal was to reform their own city of Kandahar. Most say they never intended to govern the country and had no political platform, Islamic or otherwise. When they took power, they tried to run the country as a military camp, by issuing decrees. That was easier than tackling the infrastructure and dealing with a plummeting standard of living.

As for Al-Qaeda, most Muslim scholars agree they are also politicians with an agenda and are using violence to advance that agenda—and religion to justify the violence. Their aim is to free Palestine and stop what they see as American occupation of Saudi Arabia.

"They aren't the only ones doing that," says Elmasry. "The U.S. has a political agenda in securing the oil supply in the Middle East. They use violence in Iraq and the occupation of Saudi Arabia to impose that agenda. They advance the political agenda by military means and justify it by saying [Saddam] Hussein is evil."

Elmasry blames the downfall of Islam seven hundred years ago on the fact that the Muslim people stopped following the teachings of tolerance and moderate living, and ceased the championing of human rights, freedom of religion and cooperation. "It was a cycle in civilization. Any civilization that doesn't stick to high morals and the human dignity of its doctrines will decay."

The debate about Islam today suggests that change is on the agenda. Women are part of that change. For all the accusations being hurled at the religion, it is interesting to note that Islam has more converts, especially women, than any other religion today.

Those women may be the paradigm shift needed to close the gap between the hallowed fundamentals of Islam and the fundamentalist extremism that has sidelined women and tarnished Islam. Feminists and liberation theologians have applied what has been termed "a hermeneutic of suspicion," as they approach traditional religious interpretation. They ask the question, Whose interests does this interpretation serve? They contend that traditional interpretations serve the power interests of patriarchy and socio-economic-political forces currently holding power. In other words, the interpretations maintain the status quo. They are usually correct.

An example of this travesty is the claim that was traditionally made for Biblical validation of apartheid in South Africa. Liberation theologians demolished the pro-apartheid interpretation of Romans 13.

Feminist theory sees authority in the Christian and Jewish religions as one of domination, resting in the hands of whoever has control. Feminist Muslim scholars have recently started examining the Koran, using the same principles. If Islam is to have a reformation, the women will be part of it. But separating the secular and the public may be too large a shift for a religion that views its spiritual and social life as one, guided by the same laws. Any change, particularly for Afghanistan, needs to come from Muslim women themselves.

Chapter 5

THE VEILED THREAT OF MISOGYNY

The Taliban didn't invent misogyny. For centuries, men have controlled, bullied and scapegoated women in the name of tradition or religious orthodoxy: foot-binding in China, honor-killing in the Middle East and much of Asia, female genital mutilation in Africa, bride-burning in India. In North America, laws have kept women in financial purdah and sexual fear, and religious fundamentalists have kept women from participating in civil society. Women have paid a terrible price for the willful misinterpretations of religion and the cultural role society has assigned them.

All societies are divided along gender lines. For most societies, the public world is a world of work, where men exert most of the power; the private world, on the other hand, is a world of family, a world of women. The division shapes the lives of women and exposes them to cultural practices and beliefs that are historically produced, socially constructed and culturally defined. Breaking out of that bind is a challenge. For the most part, women have been thwarted in their efforts to overcome the male-centered power in their lives. International laws and human-rights conventions have failed to rescue half the world's population from the sometimes life-threatening ties that bind a woman to her father or husband.

In much of the world, there is a bizarre duality: the perception of women as fragile creatures who need protection, or as evil Jezebels from whom society needs protection. A mullah in Bangladesh judges a woman indecent because she wants to work and earn money to feed her children. A judge in Canada finds a man not guilty of sexual assault because the woman he attacked was "not exactly wearing a bonnet and crinolines." The woman in Bangladesh is ostracized. The woman in Canada is ridiculed.

Women are identified with feelings rather than reason, with their bodies rather than their minds. In many countries, the girl child is victimized by the same misogyny that affects her mother. She's fed last and least. She's denied education and saddled with the responsibility of household chores, while her brothers go out to play. In India, female babies are sometimes starved to death so families can avoid financially crushing dowry payments; girls are burned to death as teenage brides because their husbands want to get rid of them for a better dowry. In China, they are abandoned or dropped to their deaths from a tower simply because boys are preferred in the one-child-per-family policy in China. In Peru and Mexico, they're sold into slavery, and in Bangladesh they're sometimes told at the tender age of five and six to leave home and make their own way. They join thousands of other girls in the streets looking for something to eat, trying to stay alive. And in Canada, where women boast charter rights, street prostitutes are often young girls escaping abuse—usually sexual abuse—at home.

Just as it was women around the world who rallied to support the women of Afghanistan, women's groups are fighting misogyny in numerous places around the world. The model they would do well to follow is that of a small group of women in China who formed the Healthy Foot Society at the end of the nineteenth century and succeeded in eradicating foot-binding.

The key to their success was to make public declarations that included all women; in that way no one woman could be singled out for punishment for breaking the cultural norm. While legions of diplomats and foreign interlopers had tried to bring an end to the thousand-year-old foot-binding practice, which deformed and crippled girls at about the age of five, all attempts to stop it had failed. When the women in the Healthy Foot Society realized that other people, field workers for example, didn't bind their daughters' feet, that there was no justification of this practice in their religion or their culture, they issued a public declaration that said, "I will never bind my daughter's feet and I will never allow my son to marry a woman whose feet are bound." In less than a decade, the custom was ended.

Like foot-binding, female genital mutilation—the practice of cutting off the external genitalia of girls, either all or some of it, depending on the custom of the geographical area—is also a thousand-year-old custom. It affects 130 million women around the world, and every day six thousand girls between the ages of four and twelve are added to the list of those who suffer the agony of FGM in much of North, West and East Africa and parts of Asia. For the rest of their lives, the health of these girls will be compromised because of a custom that has no religious basis and no explanation for how it found its way into the culture. What makes the situation worse is that there is a taboo about speaking of the procedure.

But the women in the small village of Malicounda in Senegal, West Africa, rebelled. When they discovered that other women around the world and even in some nearby villages weren't subjected to FGM, that their own health problems were caused by what had been done to them as little girls, they banded together. Like the Chinese women fighting to stop foot-binding, they made a public declaration: "Never again, not my daughter." Women's groups in other African countries are following their lead. Some say FGM will be eradicated within five years.

Honor-killing—when male relatives kill women who are perceived to have tarnished the family's reputation—is another widespread example of misogyny. Women living on the West Bank in Jordan, in Brazil, or in other countries where the law says that killing a wife or female relative is justifiable if she brings dishonor to the family, are also fighting back. The so-called honor crimes have included cases in which a husband orders his wife to turn over her wages to him, otherwise, he'll tell the neighbors that she has been unfaithful—an accusation that will ensure her a death sentence. Women in Jordan twice petitioned parliament to demand the law be changed. Led by lawyer Asma Khader and Sisterhood Is Global Institute (SIGI), the women are preparing to return to parliament, and this time they expect a victory. On the West Bank, the fight to change the law is being led by Nadera Shalhoub-Kevorkian.

Venerable institutions such as the World Bank and the North-South Institute are also endorsing socially progressive policies. These organizations have declared that rich countries would see more positive social and economic change if they invested in the girl child. Their reports state that with food, education and health care, the girl child will stay at home longer, marry later, have fewer children, and that those children will be healthier. They argue that those changes alone would drastically alter the economic inequities, and that it is the girl child who can eradicate poverty, save the environment and put a country to work. The reports, published in the mid-1990s, were heralded as progressive—and then mostly ignored. But women's organizations around the world are using them as a clarion call.

Women like Dr. Samar in Afghanistan, Nadera Shalhoub Kevorkian on the West Bank, Asma Khader in Jordan, and the women of Malicounda in Senegal are sowing the seeds of change.

During the summer of 1998, I visited the women of Malicounda to find out how they managed to eradicate a tradition that had ruled their lives and wrecked their health. We met in a small room that the women had constructed themselves and painted a delicate yellow for the literacy classes they planned to conduct. The contrast in the room was stunning: the beauty and serenity of the women sitting in the circle; the brutality of the stories they shared. It was in this little meeting room that they learned that the ancient ritual of excision (female circumcision) performed on them as little girls was the cause of the chronic health problems they suffer as adults. It was here they learned that cutting off a girl's external genitalia had nothing to do with religion. And it was here they made a public declaration to forever ban a thousand-year-old ethnic tradition.

The women of Malicounda, a village of about three thousand, are far away from the cosmopolitan offices of worldly bureaucrats. But here, amid the clusters of thatched-roof huts, herds of bleating goats and towering baobab trees, they had succeeded where diplomats, politicians and scores of Western women had failed. They made history as the first village to stop

performing female genital mutilation. Today, the movement
they started is spreading like a grass fire across Senegal and
into neighboring countries.

Given the taboo about speaking of the custom wherever it is
practiced, it was with some trepidation that Dr. Winnie Tay, the
director of Plan International in Sierra Leone, organized the
country's first conference on female genital mutilation in May
1996. Today, in his new office in Senegal, Tay recalls that the
vice-president of Sierra Leone was supposed to give the
opening address, but canceled at the last minute. "Later, he said
to me, 'As a medical doctor, I support you. As a politician, I
can't touch this.'"

Tay's gamble paid off. The conference hall was packed. The
taboo subject was at last at the debating table. "Culture and
tradition are waging a silent yet devastating war on girl children," he told the attendees, who included sociologists, aid
workers, religious leaders, teenagers and their fathers and
mothers. The audience sat in horrified silence as they watched
a videotape depicting the graphic details of the procedure
recorded in Ethiopia. The child in the video is eight years old.
Today is her birthday. Her mother takes her by the hand and
leads her to a hut at the edge of the village. Inside the hut she
is tied to a chair, with her legs splayed. An old woman clutch-
ing a rusty razor tells her to be brave and not to make a noise.
Then she grasps the skin above the child's clitoris and begins
cutting. The child screams in agony while the woman slices off
piece after piece: the hood of the clitoris, the clitoris itself, the
labia minora, the labia majora. She closes the gaping bloody
wound with three thorns and slathers it with what looks like
herbs and raw eggs. The child is removed to a mat, her legs are
tied together and she's told that now she is a woman.

If she doesn't bleed to death, if she doesn't die from shock
or pelvic infection or tetanus, she faces a lifetime of pain.
The opening she's left with is the size of the tip of the little

finger. Passing urine is so painful, she'll try to retain it, which causes urinary tract infection and sometimes septicemia. When she's old enough to menstruate, she'll suffer again as the menstrual flow pools inside the scarred wall simply because it can't exit through the tiny opening. And when she marries and is re-cut with a razor to make intercourse possible, she faces the added burden of becoming pregnant with a birth canal that has been mutilated. She'll adopt the expression so many women before her have learned: "The first one always dies. It is making a passage for the other children." Because the labia minora that stretches and aids in a baby's birth has been cut off, the labor is prolonged and the baby is often starved of oxygen.

The participants at the symposium were thunderstruck. The men claimed they had no idea what was being done to their wives and daughters. In fact, the women themselves didn't know the details—only their own memories of the experience—as it was not a subject they could discuss with anyone. Now, after viewing the shocking images, people in that Sierre Leone conference hall wanted to talk.

The roots of this brutal rite of passage are as confounding as the business of stopping it. Some say it is a religious requirement, but although it is practiced by both Muslims and Christians and a Jewish sect in Ethiopia, it is not mentioned in either the Koran or the Bible. Some say it is to improve the health and child-bearing capabilities of the women, despite irrefutable medical evidence to the contrary. Others claim it is to make a woman more attractive, a better wife and more sexually satisfied. In fact, it hobbles a woman with scarring, pain and sexual trauma. Still others claim that, like foot-binding in China and other misogynist practices, it stems from an obsession with purity, sanctioned by tradition.

The United Nations had tried for more than a decade to stop FGM. World courts made it a criminal offense—so have many of the countries where it is practiced. Western women have descended on the villages with accusations of barbarism. But until the women of Malicounda set an example in July 1997, village women ignored the UN, refused to obey a law that trod on their ancient customs and essentially told Western women to go home and mind their own business.

A few months after the declaration by the women of Malicounda, twelve more villages took the same oath. Then in June of 1998 eighteen villages in the southern region of Kolda, in Senegal—people of the Faluni and Mandinka ethnic groups—also declared a ban on FGM. In October women in the neighboring country of Mali invited the women of Malicounda to come to discuss the business of declaring an end to FGM. And in the St. Louis district, north of Senegal's capital, Dakar, another seventy villages made their declaration public on November 22, 1999.

The Senegal initiative is one of those "overnight" success stories that was seven years in the making. By all accounts, the story began with Molly Melching, a woman from small-town USA (Danville, Illinois) who went to Dakar twenty-four years ago as an exchange student and never went home. She learned the language, adopted the styles of the people, moved into a village and, in the process, experienced an epiphany: change isn't an external event, it's an internal event. "Given the opportunity to gather the information needed for change, you'll make the decision yourself," says Melching, a six-foot-tall charismatic woman who fills the room with her presence. "And if it's your idea, it'll work."

In 1991 Melching started a non-government organization called Tostan, which means "breakthrough" in the native Wolof language. She developed a six-part program for women that included basic hygiene, literacy and problem-solving. She knew the dropout rate in literacy classes was very high and felt that if she could make the classroom a nurturing place where women wanted to be, where they could talk about issues important to them, they would stay. She uses story-telling, songs and theatre as her teaching tools. Soon enough the women told her they wanted to learn about their own health, their bodies. "I realized they didn't know about menstruation, about menopause, about parts of their bodies. What it came down to was they didn't know what their rights were. When I told them about human rights and that they had the right to health, we began to have incredible conversations. They discussed wife assault for the first time. They talked about child labor and discovered that the children had the right to education, to being with their parents, and shouldn't be sent off at the age of ten to work as maids in the towns. Then I asked them what problems they had with excision [FGM] They said, 'None.' So I asked if we shouldn't talk about it. 'Yes, talk about it,' they said. 'But you'll never ever change it.'"

Until then, when health workers asked women who had been circumcised if they had problems with, for example, urinating or delivering babies, they would say no. They assumed it was normal to take fifteen minutes to urinate and three to five days of hard labor to deliver a baby. When the women in Melching's classes began to realize that other women didn't experience the health problems they did, the floodgates opened. Women shared their stories and drew the inevitable conclusion: they needed to make changes.

But change, particularly one that dismantles a thousand-year-old ritual, comes at a cost. Soon after the women banished FGM, the inevitable backlash followed. They had agreed to allow reporters from Dakar to come to the village and ask questions. On July 31, 1997, their story headlined every newspaper in the country. The month of August bore witness to the perilous path of pioneers. The newspapers portrayed them as revolutionaries. Some religious leaders scorned the women. Their husbands accused them of having no *satura* (discretion) by speaking publicly about such a private and culturally sensitive issue. And some militant defenders of cultural identity called down a pox on their houses.

The women called a meeting, a return to the circle in the little yellow room where they'd met weekly for two years. When Melching arrived and talked to the women, she was truly worried about them. "You have already suffered enough," she told them. "You could go back. You could change your mind. Or you could stop talking to others about the decision you made. This backlash could get worse."

Silence.

Then Tene Cissiko, a thirty-one-year-old mother of four, stood up. The tension in the room was palpable. All eyes turned to the attractive woman who, like her ancestors, had never before questioned FGM. "No," she said. "We'll never go back. We made this decision based on what we know to be true. We are Amazon women. We'll continue the struggle even if it means problems."

Every woman in the room stood with her. And like apostles of their newly discovered human rights, they began to spread the word. When the village of Ker Simbara was preparing for its annual circumcision rites, the Malicounda women traveled the sixty-kilometer (thirty-seven-mile) distance to tell the village women why they had decided to stop the tradition. They knew that sharing their knowledge with the women wasn't enough. They needed to talk to the men, the elders and the Imam (the Muslim leader of the area).

Initially, the people of Ker Simbara were furious. But the Imam, an old man called Demba Diawara, was upset by the stories he heard that day. Could it be true? he wondered. He told the women, "We are a family of eleven villages. We could never do this without talking to the rest of our family."

Speaking in the epigrammatic style he favors, Diawara explained to me, "Your brain always has two voices. One will give you advice. One will stop you from changing. I thought I had to listen to this new information. But I also thought our traditions need to be respected. I felt it was my obligation at that point to put on my shoes and go and talk to the rest of our family about this."

He and his nephew, Chiekh Traore, trekked village to village. They met with the chief, the leader of the women's group and the young people. "We didn't just go once. We went back three or four times. These things had never been discussed publicly." Traore adds, "I went and talked to a medical doctor about what the women were saying. He said, 'This is something you practice but it is very detrimental to the health of women and girls.' He gave me examples and it all began to make sense to me. We'd heard stories we couldn't believe. If we'd known this before, we would have stopped excision a long time ago."

On November 20, 1997, the president of Senegal, Abdou Diouf, made a declaration of his own. "I want all the villages of Senegal to follow the example set by the women of Malicounda." On February 3, 1998, he began the process of writing the ban into the law of the land.

While social anthropologists have always believed it would take hundreds of years to end FGM, research fellows like Gerry Mackie, an academic at Oxford University in England who has written extensively about the end of foot-binding in China, says that this no longer holds true. In fact, says Mackie, because of the method used by Melching, "It will end suddenly and universally."

He uses the Chinese Healthy Foot Society to illustrate why. Foot-binding was the custom of folding a little girl's toe under her foot, bending the arch down, virtually breaking it, and binding the foot so it wouldn't grow, presumably making the girl delicate and fragile and therefore appealing to men. It certainly stopped her from running away, as she couldn't walk more than a few feet, and even that was done with great difficulty. It persisted in China for a thousand years, but once reform began, it ended in about nine. "The work of foot-binding reformers had three aspects," says Mackie. "First, they carried out a modern education campaign, which explained that the rest of the world did not bind women's feet. Second, they explained the advantage of natural feet and the disadvantage of bound feet. Third, they formed natural foot societies whose members publicly pledged not to bind their daughters' feet, nor to let their sons marry women with bound feet. The women of Malicounda reinvented the techniques of the foot-binding reformers when they took part in the Tostan program." The key, he says, is the public pledge and the fact that Tostan provides the education but never tells people what to do.

Molly Melching was delighted if somewhat overwhelmed by the rapid-fire success of her program. The program spread across Senegal, and six neighboring countries asked for Tostan's assistance.

On the road to eliminating a practice that has been a scourge to African women, she has also experienced her share of the backlash. One man spit on her in Dakar. Another shrieked obscenities at "the woman who is destroying our traditions." But mostly Melching is received like family by an ever-increasing number of Senegalese people who see her as their hero.

One is Ibrahima Ndiaye, office manager at a large European airline in Dakar. "When I got married, my wife and I couldn't have intercourse because she was closed. I knew this was done to women, but I'd never given any thought to the conse-quences. Then her aunt came and opened her up with a razor. I couldn't believe what was happening. My wife was in terrible pain. I vowed that such a thing would never be done to my daughters. We had six daughters and one son. When the first two girls were little, my wife's aunt kept telling me they had to be cut or they'd never be accepted at the village. I said, 'Too bad. They'll never be cut.' Then one day I came home from work and I knew the moment I opened the door that something was wrong. The aunt was there. My wife's face was a mask of fear. Usually my little girls—they were two and four at the time—came running to the door to greet me. They weren't there. I asked my wife what was going on. She said, 'They're in the bedroom.' I rushed in and there were my little daughters lying on the bed, their legs bound by bloody robes. I was furious. I wanted to call the police, but the aunt said, 'Go ahead, they won't do anything. This is our tradition.' She had come with the excisist while I was at work and said to my wife, 'We're here to do the girls.' We didn't have a phone. There was nothing my wife could do. The aunt said, 'Maybe you're angry now, but you'll thank me when it's time for them to marry because no man will have a girl who is not excised.' I told her that any man who wanted to marry my daughter because she was excised would never have my permission. He can marry her for love, never for excision."

Back in Malicounda, we sat again in the meeting room, and this time the tropical storm raging outside was for real. It was the rainy season in Senegal, the first rainy season that didn't mark the completion of circumcision rights of girls. Everybody wanted to talk about the pride, courage and confidence they had gathered since their decision. But first they shared the indignation and pain they felt when they were accused of hurting their daughters. They explained, "This was our tradition. If a girl was not circumcised, she would be an outcast in the village. She could not wash with the others, prepare food with the others. She could not marry. The other children would see her as unclean."

The lessons with Melching changed all that. For Tacko Cissoko, a midwife who attends births in her own ethnic group, which practices FGM, as well as those ethnic groups that do not, the penny dropped when they discussed childbirth. "I saw the women during delivery. The women who weren't excised didn't tear. The women who were, tore terribly. I always suspected excision was the cause." The women speak as one when they say, "This is a chance for our daughters. They won't have to suffer. They won't lose their health. They won't spend all their money on health problems when they're adults."

They know it's about power, the power to decide for yourself—a paradigm shift for women. By taking a stand, the women of Malicounda began to dismantle the ancient tradition, a bold move that's being emulated throughout Africa.

In December 1999, I visited Nadera Shalhoub-Kevorkian in Jerusalem and on the West Bank, to find out how murder was legally sanctioned as honor-killing. She's been tracking cases of honor-killing from her cramped office at Hebrew University in Jerusalem since 1993. Her bookshelves are stacked with petitions and scholarly papers that chronicle the sometimes life-threatening ties that bind a woman to her father or husband in Arab society. And her filing cabinets are jammed with the brutal statistics of honor-killing, an ancient custom that is practiced by both Muslims and Christians on the West Bank, in Gaza, among Israeli Arabs, across the river in Jordan, and to a greater or lesser extent throughout the Middle East and parts of Asia as well as in Brazil.

One of the files was about a girl called Samera. Flirting proved a costly mistake for Samera. She was fifteen years old when her neighbors in Salfeet, a small Palestinian town on the West Bank, saw her chatting with a young man. Since she had been without a male chaperone, her family's honor was at stake; a marriage was quickly arranged. By sixteen, she had a child. Five years later, when she could stand the bogus marriage no longer, she bolted. In a place where a girl's sexual life is as public as her name, Samera's actions were considered shameful. According to the gossips, she went from man to man as she moved from place to place. Finally, her family caught up with her. A few days later she was found stuffed down a well. Her neck had been broken. Her father told the coroner she'd committed suicide. But everyone knew that Samera was a victim of honor-killing, murdered by her own family because her actions brought dishonor to their name.

Nadera Shalhoub-Kevorkian, a passionate advocate for Palestinian women's rights, knew it too. She marched into the coroner's office and demanded an autopsy. Charges were laid against Samera's father and brother. But Shalhoub-Kevorkian knows they'll never stick. Here in the West Bank, the Palestinian Authority's law allows honor-killing. Samera's parents walk the streets of their neighborhood with their heads held high, relieved that the family honor has been restored.

Shalhoub-Kevorkian continues to take cases such as Samera's to court, demanding answers. In doing so, she's cracking a code of silence that has kept some rural and uneducated women under virtual house arrest and, in extreme cases, paying with their lives for the family's so-called honor. It's a code that also silences urban educated women who may be spared death but live their lives with the suffocating threat of their own vulnerability.

According to police reports, twenty-three Palestinian women on the West Bank and in Gaza were victims of honor-killings in 1999. In Jordan twenty-six more reportedly suffered the same fate. Tribal chiefs, the keepers of the cultural key in places such as the West Bank and Jordan, admit it's actually ten times that number. Women who've been raped, who are judged promiscuous, who refuse an arranged marriage, or have simply become expendable to husbands whose honor would be

besmirched by admitting they want a divorce, may be elimi-
nated. They are bashed over the head, shot, choked to death,
mutilated and then erased from the family history. Hundreds
more women are in hiding. A shelter system is in its infancy, so
women who dare to seek refuge are being held in jails for their
own safety, sharing their lives with murderers to escape the
lethal plotting of their own families.

The obsession with the purity of women has survived for
centuries. This new century may finally bring its demise. The
issue of the emancipation of women is thrusting itself even into
this conservative corner of the planet. A sisterhood of Arab
women in groups such as SIGI and the association of Women
Living Under Muslim Laws is banding together, defying the
law, rescuing women and stashing them in safe havens while
they lobby for change. They've been accused of promoting
promiscuity and destroying the traditional family.

"Don't talk to me about honor-killing," says activist
Shalhoub-Kevorkian, stabbing the table with a stir stick to
emphasize her point at the faculty club of the Hebrew
University. "The two words don't go together. In the West, you
call it crimes of passion. Here, it's called crimes of honor. It's
neither. This is 'femicide,' the killing of women."

A criminologist, social worker and assistant professor,
Shalhoub-Kevorkian is a woman with Sophia Loren good
looks and boundless energy for the blitzkrieg she's launched
against the enemy. A Palestinian of Christian Orthodox faith,
she delivers eloquent testimonials—on the Arab culture she
adores, on the violence against women she abhors, and on half
a dozen cases she's involved in. "I love my culture and I know
how to change what's wrong with it. I don't have stones to
throw politically. My stones are to empower women, to build
a safe service for them." On March 8, 2000, International
Women's Day, Shalhoub-Kevorkian hosted the first Palestinian
conference on femicide.

She started with a hotline in 1993, soon after one of her students told her that his cousin had been raped. When she tried to intervene to help the girl, she discovered that no one wanted to know about it, not her family, not even the hospital staff. In fact, there were no shelters, no counseling services, no support whatsoever. Soon after the hotline was established, one of the first calls recorded the pathetic cries of a ten-year-old girl: "I was alone in the house one day when our neighbor, Wajeeh, knocked on the door wanting to borrow some sugar. I opened the door because we borrow back and forth all the time. But in the kitchen, he wrestled me to the ground, pulled down my skirt and pants and did something very painful to me. While he was on his way out, my mother and eldest brother came home. They both started beating me. They were both yelling *'Inshallah tmuti'*—It's best for you to die. The child became a prisoner in her home until she was fourteen and old enough to be married off to the offending Wajeeh. She never saw her playmates or attended school again, and to this day blames herself for opening the door. It's cases such as these that propelled Shalhoub-Kevorkian to take on the system, to create the social unit at the Women's Center for Legal Aid and Counseling in Jerusalem, to enlist the support of social workers, psychologists and lawyers. To get a meeting with the mufti (an Islamic religious leader) to discuss a case, she persuaded several male business leaders and professors to go with her. "I just needed men—500 kilos is usually enough—so I could get the meeting."

Women who struggle to change the status quo for women invariably pay a price for breaking the silence of a tribal custom. When Shalhoub-Kevorkian commented publicly on the case of a seventeen-year-old girl who'd been gang-raped, she wound up on the evening news demanding, "What are this girl's choices? She can marry the rapist or some sixty-five-year-old man who will remove her shame, or she can be imprisoned all the rest of her life in the house, or she can be killed. *Ya bitmout, ya bitmout, ya bitmout*—either she dies or she dies or she dies." A few days later Shalhoub-Kevorkian's car was stopped on the road between the West Bank city of Ramallah and Jerusalem. Three men yanked her out, grabbed her by the throat, beat her with sticks driven with nails and fled. She got the message but won't back down. "You can't just talk the talk on this issue; you have to walk the walk as well."

She explains: "Our society is in transition. The codes of conduct aren't clear. Some people are trying to move backward to preserve the norm; others are moving forward. In the process, there's more attention to crimes against women, more willingness to help, more cases of women being killed and more fear."

The poisonous root of honor-killing is centuries old, dating to the pre-Islamic era called Jahiliyah (the Time of Ignorance Before Muhammad) when men were encouraged to bury infant daughters alive to avoid the possibility that they would grow up to dishonor the family. Scholars of Islam say this practice has nothing to do with the Koran and that, in fact, the prophet Muhammad called for an end to burying girls. Instead, honor-killing has burgeoned and sent deadly tentacles into much of Asia. In Pakistan, Afghanistan and Iran, women are stoned to death for infidelity—and in India and Bangladesh, they are burned alive in "sari fires" for such crimes as being an unsuitable bride.

The law in the West Bank and Jordan states that killing is justifiable when a man finds his wife or female relative fornicating with another man. If he kills her based on suspicion alone, he must explain himself in court. Variations of the same law serve in Gaza and the rest of the Middle East. But these are justice systems in which four adult male witnesses are required to convict a man of adultery or rape; the testimony of women is excluded. The law in the West Bank also allows men to bury

their dead daughters and go to the police station after the fact
to fill in a death certificate, naming whatever cause of death
they choose.

What is central is public "knowing"—the need to take
action to save face. If the "crime" is not known, there's no pressure to take action. But if it's made public, a girl's life becomes
the tool to censor the gossips and rescue the family's honor.
Arab culture casts the male as the sole protector of the female,
so he must have total control of her. If his protection is
violated, he loses honor because either he failed to protect her
or he failed to bring her up correctly.

Women like Samera pay the ultimate price for this failure.
Today her little black dunnage bag with the propitious logo
"Passport" splashed in purple across the side sits unclaimed in
the Women's Center. It's filled with all her worldly goods: an
overcoat, a chador, the greeting cards she designed and sold to
make a living, and a photo of her little girl.

Samera's champion, Shalhoub-Kevorkian, says death is
only one form of femicide living with the threat of death
for your entire life is another. In the Arab world, she says,
femicide comes in four forms. First, there is the unspoken
threat—external social controls such as not going to school,
staying at home or in an enforced marriage. The second is
the active threat to kill. The third is the act of trying to kill
a daughter. West Bank hospitals, shelters and even jails—
where victims are stashed for their own protection—bear
witness to the walking wounded who survive a murderous
attack. And the fourth is actually murdering a woman and
getting away with it.

Getting away with it is disturbingly easy. Dr. Jalal Aljabri,
director of the Forensic Medical Center for the Palestinian
Authority in East Jerusalem, says he hardly ever sees a case in
which honor-killing is the official cause of death. "In our
culture, everybody knows but nobody says. I get cases that say

the cause of death is a firearm injury. I know inside what really happened but what can I do? I sign the certificate and say, 'Bye-bye; that's it.'"

Dr. Aljabri exemplifies the "enlightened" Palestinian man. Ask him about the price women sometimes pay for safeguarding the family's name and he's strongly against honor-killing. Ask him about his own family and the tone changes. He's the father of eight, five boys and three girls. What would he do if one of his daughters became pregnant and wasn't married? He's aghast at the question. "A girl knows she cannot be pregnant. She cannot have sexual relations. She must understand what would happen."

So, what would he do? "I don't know," he replies.

His counterpart in Jordan, Dr. Hani Jahshan, thinks encouraging women's rights and equality is the way to solve the problem. Dr. Jahshan recounts case after case of women who turned up on his autopsy table, victims of honor-killing. "Women are brought to me to be examined after a sexual assault. I tell their parents they are innocent, but a few weeks later I see them again, dead." The crime is not about rape or murder. The crime is loss of chastity.

In the cosmopolitan Jordanian capital of Amman, the women's organization Sisterhood Is Global Institute (SIGI) went to the courts in 1999 and demanded that Jordan's government change the law to make sentences for honor-killing commensurate with those for murder. Its plea was rejected almost unanimously by the Jordanian parliament. But Asma Khader, the leader of the group, says the organization will return to the parliament, this time with the support of several Christian and Muslim religious leaders as well as King Abdullah, his wife, Queen Rania, and the hugely popular Queen Noor, widow of the late King Hussein.

"I think we may get it this time," Khader says. But she knows changing the law isn't enough. "We need a public-awareness campaign. We need to send a cultural message to the people that this isn't acceptable anymore."

The campaign will need to include the very young, since boys and girls alike are taught that the hymen is the center of the family's honor. Dr. Salwa Al-Najjab, an obstetrician/gynecologist in Ramallah, who is also on the board at the Women's Center for Legal Aid and Counseling, says, "I was just eleven years old when my mother told me about the hymen being like a glass; if it's broken it can never hold water again. She didn't even tell me about menstruation. Just about hymens."

Every day at Dr. Al-Najjab's clinic, someone seeks information about the state of a girl's hymen. People here still believe that a woman must bleed after intercourse on her wedding night as proof of her virginity. One doctor who doesn't want to be named, says, "If I'm asked to examine a girl to check if her hymen is in place, I always say it is. Why would I say otherwise if I know they will kill her?" If a doctor does disclose the damning truth and if the family has financial resources, they may choose to spare the girl's life by seeking hymen repair surgery—stitching the sides of the hymen together. Dr. Al-Najjab calls it an "unethical money-making business that exploits women."

In their struggle for change, Dr. Al-Najjab and her colleagues found a correlation between political power and emancipation. "During the intifada (the Palestinian uprising against Israel in the late 1980s and early '90s) women were seen as partners. The young women and men passed out pamphlets, threw stones and worked on the street together. At that time, the killing of women decreased," she said. "But when there was no change in the political situation, the women went back to their houses. Now, if they're on the street, they're seen as women, not as partners, and the rate of femicide has increased."

The task of undoing a centuries-old custom is a monumental undertaking. Resistance comes from many quarters:

tribal chiefs, for example, who put governments into power and allow monarchies such as the one in Jordan to rule, would forfeit their role as cultural power-brokers. Religious leaders would also have to bow to popular rule, not a comfortable position for those whose word has been law for centuries.

A week before Christmas Eve 1999, Shalhoub-Kevorkian and I left Jerusalem to drive to a meeting of the board of the Women's Center being held in Ramallah. The city was overflowing with tourists celebrating the last Christmas of the millennium. The twinkling decorations and the robes of the priests and mullahs on the street served as a poignant reminder about the origins of this Holy Land. But suddenly, as we drove by the Dung Gates to the Old City, Shalhoub-Kevorkian stopped the car and said, "Look, see the village by the gates? That's Silwan. In October three women were killed in that village for so-called honor crimes. Now, there's social panic. Even very little girls are wearing veils. They're scared to death."

In Ramallah, the women gathered in a hotel meeting room. They went through an agenda aimed at establishing shelters, new laws and empowerment for women and girls. Outside, as the sun dropped over a rocky hill in ancient Palestine, the wailing of the mullah on the loudspeaker in the street below called the people to prayer. This was Ramadan, the holiest month of the Islamic year. While Muslims fasted and bowed to the east, and Christians found their way to Bethlehem from Jerusalem, the women in the room upstairs were searching for strategies to save the lives of women whose men were at prayer.

In Afghanistan in 1999, the mullahs also wail their call to prayers at sunrise and sunset every day. But there are no Afghan women gathered in hotel meeting rooms or anyplace else. The women have become invisible, confined to their homes, hidden behind purdah walls, forbidden to take part in civil society. Misogyny was taking its toll, but not just on the daughters of Afghanistan. Men, women and children were facing a bleak future that would all but destroy their country.

Chapter 6

LIFE UNDER THE TALIBAN

Four years after the world's most oppressive regime began ruling Afghanistan, the daily lives of women had turned into a a test of survival. Their health was failing, the Taliban were getting bolder and the international community continued to wring its hands. In a *realpolitik* response to Afghanistan's deteriorating situation, the United Nations made accommodations with the unsavory Taliban in order to get access to the suffering people and ensure that humanitarian aid organizations wouldn't be thrown out of the country. That accommodation often meant going along with such inequities as allowing the feeding, schooling and employment of males over females.

During the fall of 2000, the United Nations suggested that as the Taliban had loosened its grip on Afghan society, the situation for the people was improving. In monthly reports and in response to reporters' questions, the UN pointed out that some education for girls was permitted, that some women were working in the health-care field and even that the vast poppy production—which made Afghanistan the source of 70 percent of the world's heroin supply—had halted.

My ongoing communication with Dr. Sima Samar and the refugee women who had left the country during the last five years made me wonder how such a conclusion could have been reached. As for the cultivation of the poppy, by 1999 the drought in Afghanistan had continued into a third year. Nothing was growing, not poppies, not wheat; even the ancient almond trees had withered and died.

Then in December 2000 I received an anonymous letter, smuggled out of Afghanistan, from a woman in Kandahar. She said, "As an Afghan woman, I am deeply concerned about the recent reports claiming that restrictions on women are slowly being lifted. These reports that progress is being made in Afghanistan do not accurately portray the horrible lives of women today under the Taliban. The UN officials and humanitarian aid organizations who are making these claims are not living under the Taliban's restrictions. They are highly respected by the Taliban and can do whatever they want in Afghanistan. [In Kandahar] they live in big houses and have very good salaries and servants. If they had to live in the country as Afghan women with their daughters, they would never accept these restrictions and they would never describe them as cultural."

In the winter of 2001, I decided to travel to Kandahar, the spiritual capital of the Taliban, to see for myself.

Gaining entrance to this place as a woman, a journalist and a foreigner—all red flags to the ruling Taliban—required patience and downright chicanery. Since getting an eyewitness report on the status of women was not considered an acceptable reason for entering the country, I needed to invent a cover. I had learned several months earlier that Canada was funding a non-government organization called Guardians, which was doing excellent work at the Institute for Orthopaedics in Kandahar. I thought there might be a match between its purposes and mine: they wanted publicity for the Institute and I wanted to report firsthand on how women were faring under the Taliban.

I left Toronto armed with a visa for Pakistan, knowing I'd then have to negotiate a visa for Afghanistan. My application for that visa turned into a three-day stakeout at the Taliban's administration office in Quetta. Scowling men with Kalashnikovs stood guard. Peons entered the office nervously, carrying trays of green tea. When they left the room, they backed reverentially away from the functionary I was waiting to meet.

He sat behind a large bare desk looking alternately bored and bemused. I hovered in the doorway, hoping to look subservient enough to get an audience. Suddenly he waved me into the office and, to my surprise, spoke to me in English. He proved to be utterly charming, with the good looks of a swash-buckling Hollywood movie star. He even told me he knew what the media was saying about Afghanistan because he surfed the Net! He then gave me a list of daunting tasks—papers to fill out and get signed in half a dozen different bureaus in Quetta, photos to be taken for the documents I must carry at all times. The photo in my passport was not acceptable since "the woman is smiling and the yellow hair is showing."

When I completed those tasks, I returned, only to spend another day waiting to have the papers processed; I was told to come back yet again "for discussion." When I returned, the visa was sitting on the corner of his desk, unsigned, so I realized there was another test to come. The official asked if I was familiar with the Islamic laws of his country. I decided this was probably not the place to argue about his interpretation of the Koran and simply replied, "Yes." Then he asked if I was carrying a camera. Since we were surrounded by menacing-looking men with machine guns, I replied, "Yes, but it's only a little camera." He wanted to see it. When I handed over my Pentax 115M, which is about the size of a pack of cards, he agreed and said, "It's only little, you can use it." Then he announced that because I am a woman, I could only travel if accompanied by a man.

The regional director of Guardians in Afghanistan, Zalmai Mojadidi, agreed to fill the role of requisite male. Mojadidi is like a bearded, turbaned Danny DeVito; he's got the same strut and the same savvy-but-vulnerable modus operandi. In the coming days he would show me the project he's so proud of at the Institute for Orthopaedics and steer me through a series of calamities that would include an unexpected stay at the Taliban foreign office "guest house." But first we had to get across the border.

Mojadidi and I set out by truck from northern Pakistan for a bone-crushing six-hour ride to Kandahar through the Kojak Pass and over what remains of the highway to Afghanistan. When we reached the border, it was like crossing the proverbial line in the sand. We parked the truck and walked along a dusty donkey path—between the vendors' shacks in the desert town of Spin Baldak. I trod carefully, keeping my chador wrapped around my face, concealing my hands even as they desperately worked at tucking my telltale "yellow" hair back under the chador. Ahead was a sign that had "Passport" scrawled on it in black ink over a lopsided shepherd's hut with an earthen floor—and a door so low I had to duck to half my height to get inside.

Before we entered, Mojadidi had some advice. "No say hello with your hand. Smile is okay but not so much. And no your laughing, please." We'd already had a discussion about wardrobe, and he explained that only an Afghan woman had the right to wear a burqa. I wondered how it could be considered a "right" to wear a head-to-ankle body bag with a little piece of mesh in front of the eyes. We agreed that I would wear my ankle-length heavy gray winter coat, with a huge black chador wrapped around my hips, shoulders and head, which made it difficult to see, hear and walk, not to mention climb out of a truck without showing my legs.

Mojadidi handed over my documents to the Taliban border boss and together they discussed my wish to enter the country. I was not permitted to speak. To the man in the black turban and swirling shawl, I was invisible. Before my entry visa had even been stamped, I already felt the weight of the chains that bind the lives of women in Afghanistan.

At last the boyish-looking Talib sitting in the hut issued the requisite slip of paper that required me to report to the foreign office in Kandahar. We returned to the truck, crossed the border, and Mojadidi, my Danny DeVito fixer, whispered, "Welcome to my Afghanistan, country of tragedy."

The Taliban claimed that their strict measures had restored peace to the country and that they were serving Islam by returning to the spiritual roots of the people. In some ways, they had wrestled a dubious peace in a country that had seen two decades of civil war. Their roots were in the city of Kandahar where, in 2001, they were sharing space with Osama bin Laden, who was already known as an infamous villain who operated terrorist training camps in Afghanistan.

As we drove into Kandahar, donkey carts, sheep herds, Russian-made cars and the ubiquitous evidence of conflict— big SUVs with UN written on the doors—jockeyed for space on the dusty roads. Surprisingly, some women walked alone on the street, covered in their burqas but without the required male relative accompanying them. And some women were working in the hospital sustained by foreign aid. I heard that, in Kabul, platform shoes and even the odd pedicured toenail peeked out from under the burqas. The electricity worked most of the time. And the days of gun-slinging, robbery and rape—in broad daylight on the streets of Kandahar—seemed to be over. A nursing school had opened with fifty girls and fifty boys as students, although when I went to visit, no one was there. That became a familiar response: No students today, no patients today, no visas today—come back tomorrow. A few private home schools for girls were being tolerated.

By the beginning of 2001, the hard facts were these: most educated people had left the country. The education that did exist was limited to Koranic teachings. The vast majority of people in positions of power could not read or write. Doctors claimed that depression was endemic, diseases like tuberculosis, polio and measles were running rampant. Family planning was not allowed, and maternity health care was almost non-existent. Life expectancy had dropped to forty years. And in four years of absolute rule, the Taliban government had done nothing to rebuild the country's infrastructure or raise the desperately poor standard of living. Rather than rebuilding the roads or inoculating the population against measles and dealing with other preventable diseases, it concentrated on issuing ever more hateful edicts for women.

Things were not getting better in Afghanistan. Women told me they operated their home schools despite the unpredictable actions of the Taliban. Although the Taliban knew the schools were open, the teachers never knew when the police—from the Department for the Propagation of Virtue and Suppression of Vice—would pounce. And when they did, the teacher was jailed and the students' families were punished, usually with beatings.

The measures the Taliban took ranged from the horribly repressive to the simply ludicrous. In a state orphanage in Kabul, girls had not been allowed to leave the building since

September 1996. The boys went outside to play every day while the girls were confined to the third floor of the orphanage. Another typically ludicrous change of law was the explanation behind the ban on white socks. Initially the reason women were forbidden to wear white socks was because it was the color of the Taliban flag. Then white socks were declared sexually provocative. White socks! Since the Taliban linked the garment to sexual misconduct, the offense and therefore the punishment carried a greater penalty.

Like all totalitarian regimes, the Taliban enforced one law for the masses and another for itself. For example, although officially forbidden, music was played at some weddings, in particular at Osama bin Laden's son's nuptials. The wedding ceremony and lavish reception were held just weeks before I arrived in Kandahar. People (who would be jailed for having a party, taking photographs or watching television) witnessed a raucous party where video cameras whined and music blared until five o'clock in the morning. The people I talked to hissed bin Laden's name and his self-proclaimed Holy Man status.

What's more, the Taliban elites closed the schools, but senior Taliban administrators in Pakistan enrolled their own children in private schools. Although anyone caught smoking cigarettes was tied to a pole in a public place and faced stoning, the Taliban administrator's office that I visited was full of dirty ashtrays. The strict Shari'a law they enforced calls for the death penalty if a woman is unchaste. Yet Dr. Syada Azima, who treats refugees in the Afghan diaspora in Quetta, says, "Twenty-five percent of the women and girls over the age of thirteen that I see have sexually transmitted diseases. They get them from their husbands." The UN special rapporteur on violence against women, Radhika Coomaraswamy, visited Afghanistan in September 1999 and declared, "The international community cannot tolerate the situation in Afghanistan. No regime anywhere in the world that treats women the

Taliban way should be allowed access to the community of nations." Yet the UN officials I spoke to claimed that this kind of treatment of women was cultural, that the women always wore burqas and never went to school anyway.

The anonymous letter from the woman in Kandahar also accused the humanitarian aid agencies of misreading their mandates. "International aid agencies are saying that women will face more restrictions and suffering if the Taliban is criticized internationally for its violations of women's rights. That is not true. Humanitarian aid has not been stopped because groups have exposed the Taliban's brutalities. The Taliban's brutalities themselves are the reason so little aid is coming into Afghanistan. These international aid groups should not speak on behalf of Afghan women."

It's true that rural women do wear burqas and that only 15 percent of women are literate. It's also true that people used to think the world was flat. Progress means change. But progress in Afghanistan is seen as the face of a temptress, a role that's been fatefully assigned to women. The truly amazing thing is that resistance occurred at all. People devised coping mechanisms to keep themselves from despair. They rigged bicycle wheels as radio antennae so they could listen to the news. While television was forbidden, computers were not, so CDs provided movies and games, the only form of entertainment the people had and only because the Taliban in Kandahar hadn't figured out what the computer could deliver.

While UN officials accepted the Taliban's strictures against women as "customs," no one ever asked the women how they felt. When I returned to Quetta to visit Dr. Sima Samar's health clinic for refugees, I heard their answers. It was a Thursday so the clinic was busy. "No one comes on Wednesdays because they think if they get treatment on Wednesday the sickness will come back," explains Samar, referring to the superstitions and old wives' tales that still prevail. Outside the clinic, the silent women in line, dressed identically in their pale blue burqas, reminded me of the captive women in Margaret Atwood's *Handmaid's Tale*. But inside the curtained doorway, it was a different story. They flip back their burqas and, when asked about their lives under Taliban rule, one woman after another raged against the control men have over them. Said one, "If a Talib man wants sex with his wife, she is obliged to have it, even if she is menstruating." Another added, "I was in labor and my husband demanded sex before I went to the delivery." One woman who said she graduated from high school but cannot send her own daughter to school said flatly, "I've been wearing a burqa since I was seventeen years old. I hate it. But I have to wear it." Another described how girls in the town of Jaghori walk two hours each way to one of the clandestine schools being operated by Samar. "They don't even have proper shoes. They make the trek in plastic sandals and risk being caught by the Taliban. But attendance is 100 percent." When the Taliban came to shut down the school, they told Dr. Samar she could only educate girls until the third grade and only in Koranic teachings. Samar put a sign on the door that said "School—Grades One to Three—Koranic Teaching" and carried on with the literature, maths and science programs for girls to high-school graduation.

Dr. Samar's coping skills became as wily as the Taliban's were clumsy. One day her colleagues in Jaghori advised her that the Taliban had stolen the construction materials from her hospital. But the next day, one of their leaders in Pakistan turned up at her clinic in Quetta, demanding that Dr. Samar treat his sick mother. Samar told him, "Leave her with me overnight, I'll see what's wrong with her." When he returned to collect his mother the next day, she said, "We have a problem. You have my cement and steel. I have your mother." The materials were returned. Dr. Samar had already begun treating his mother's tonsillitis.

Dr. Samar took on all their bizarre rules and edicts and countered them at every corner. She told me a sobering story

about the Taliban decree that closed medical clinics for women.
"A woman in Hazarashat [the central region where Hazaras
live] was in labor for forty days. Her family tried to assist with
old remedies such as putting half-baked bread dough and
heated grasses on her abdomen. She was nearly dead after the
fortieth day of the ordeal when we found her. A midwife could
have diagnosed the problem easily. We did a cesarean section
and found the baby had been dead for so long the fetus and the
uterus were mixed up with necrotic tissue, and the woman
required a hysterectomy. It's incredible that she lived through
it," said Samar. "But such needless agony is unacceptable.
Furthermore, now the woman is infertile so her husband will
take another wife and she'll be relegated to servant status."

The issue of "other wives" is another point of contention
with the women. The law allows a man to have as many as four
wives; no one asks the women's opinion of this "cultural
norm." A woman who dared not have her name used told me
how humiliating it is to sleep on a mattress in one corner of the
room while your husband is with his new younger wife on a
mattress in the other corner.

Dismissing misogyny as a "cultural norm" was taking a
heavy toll on the physical and emotional health of Afghan
women and girls. Osteomalecia (a softening of the bones)
continued to plague the women. As in the West Bank and
Jordan, women are sometimes forced to undergo unnecessary
medical procedures such as the repair of a torn hymen to
satisfy Shari'a law. Samar says, "It's not unusual for a woman
to bring her daughter and ask me to check that the hymen is
intact. If it isn't, I repair it. Otherwise she will be killed."

The uneasy rhythms of life for Afghan women were evident
everywhere—from the refugee camps in Quetta to the Mirwais
Hospital compound I visited while I was in Kandahar. Just

across the road from the hospital, the Institute for Orthopaedics—with the Canadian flag pasted to the front wall—stood out like a monument amid Kandahar's destroyed buildings. It's new. It's modern by central-Asian standards, and it was treating about a thousand dismembered and disabled Afghan citizens a month. More than 700,000 Afghans are disabled. Most of the patients here showed the scars of civil war: young men missing feet and hands, arms and legs, and children maimed by some of the estimated ten million land-mines scattered throughout the country. The Canadian government stipulated that their funds were dependent on women being treated and employed as well as men. Indeed, in the basement of this two-story structure, eight women were treating disabled women who are hidden from the men upstairs.

It was there that I met secretly with a group of women in the basement to talk about their lives under the Taliban. They shed the burqas—which make them look like clones of one another—and the contrast was shocking. Under those alienating veils were pretty, vibrant, engaging women. They were teachers before the Taliban closed the schools in Kandahar. Now they were sitting behind windows painted over so no one could see them. They weren't allowed to send their own daughters to school. And although they missed the jobs they had before, all of them were grateful for the meager income this job provided.

They guided me through the work they do, introducing me to their patients. And as women do, they made the visit unforgettable, with stories about their families, kibitzing about the job, and offering me cups of the traditional green tea and delicious, hot naan bread. I noticed they wore shoes with wedges and asked why they are all the same. At first they responded as if by rote and said, "High-heeled shoes are un-Islamic." I gestured to the painted windows and asked them how they put up with this nonsense. One woman blurted out, "It's unbearable." The others quickly hushed her. Then they looked at each other and the floodgates opened. "Look at this place, it's like a jail. Women are nothing in Afghanistan today. And our shoes, they're awful. We have to wear them because the Taliban don't like the tap-tap-tap of women's high-heeled shoes. We hate having to do this." They told me of a friend who went to jail for thirty days because she invited a foreigner to a family wedding, and another who was jailed for fifteen days because she spoke to a man on the street. Their husbands were out of work. Every day was a struggle to buy enough food to feed their children. They were trying to keep their kids in the clandestine schools, but the classes were stopped so often that their education had become hit and miss, mostly miss.

I wondered how they managed to communicate with the men upstairs who do the plaster fittings of the prostheses since they could not be seen by men. They showed me the intercom system that allowed them to share their observations and instructions and said, "We know each other by the sounds of voices." Then they introduced me to Maria, an elderly woman who doesn't have to wear a burqa and was allowed to be seen by men because of her advanced age. Maria was the runner between the men's floors and the women in the basement, transferring information.

During the time I spent listening to the extraordinary events of their lives, the women and I laughed and cried together. We made friends with each other. When I left, they tucked pieces of bread and sweet cakes into my pockets for the long journey out of their country. I knew I would never forget the sweet-faced Sharifa Reza Mohseny and the good-humored, witty Frozan Mahram and her comical friend Sima Shahnawaz and the other women who worked with them. Nor would I forget their little children who were paying such a terrible price for the wreckage the merciless regime had inflicted on the country. It was truly humbling to *receive* from women who need so much to be given to them. They had the grace to worry about the comfort of someone else's voyage out of a country that had become their prison.

Leaving them behind in the basement, I went upstairs for a meeting I had arranged with the governor of Kandahar, the powerful Taliban leader called Mohammed Hasan Rahmani, who was later killed in the American bombing of Kandahar in November 2001. The juxtaposition was startling. The women I had become so fond of were stuck in a basement, their human rights stolen from them because of the man I was about to have tea with. But the governor himself was a mass of contradictions. He had warm eyes and even made a joke about the heavy winter coat and chador that I was wearing (and almost expiring in from the heat). "You are covered very well in your big Canadian burqa," he offered. "Afghan women only have to wear light burqa." He also wore a prosthesis. Rahmani had lost a limb during the Soviet occupation when, as a mujahideen fighter, he was shot in the leg; the bone became infected and an amputation was necessary. He had paid a personal price for freeing his country from the Soviets and he was genuinely perplexed by what he saw as "propaganda in foreign countries from people who lost their business here and are against the Taliban." On the topic of women, he was quick to point out, "It's totally wrong that women don't have rights. They were not safe before. Now they have possibility to go to neighbor's house and meet their relatives. More schools are coming for women but they must use Islamic religion. If any agency can help women, I want them to try."

His total disconnect on the issue of human rights was mind-numbing. He seemed to be as puzzled by the attitude of outsiders as I was by his failure to recognize his regime's misdeeds.

In the kind of *Alice through the Looking Glass* contradiction that seems to be everywhere in Afghanistan, I learned that the

Institute, besides treating victims of war and landmines, also provides prosthetics for those who have lost limbs in the grisly amputations mandated by Shari'a law. For stealing, the thief loses a hand, for stealing again, a foot. Therapist Zareen Khan was quick to point out, "The thief receives an injection of anaesthetic before the removal of the limb and so it is painless."

Not so for women who are sentenced to death by stoning for alleged illicit relations. There's no numbing her pain. In fact, the Taliban's interpretation of Shari'a law states that the stones thrown not be so big as to kill her quickly.

These punishments were meted out in the infamous Hall of Honor on the main street of Kandahar. It was here on Fridays, the holy day, that the public were told to attend the weekly punishments. At first, most people were horrified by the idea of attending the gruesome events. But eventually, as sensitivity was anaesthetized by the brutality of their everyday lives, the seats in the stadium were filled on Fridays with so-called believers who shouted bloodthirsty calls for execution.

It was increasingly obvious in early 2001 that the country was slipping into chaos. Taliban solidarity was being threatened by internal corruption and nepotism. Omar was losing control of his troops, and the devastating drought was adding to his woes. Desperation brought rules that became more ridiculous each day: pray for rain for three days and if rain doesn't come, you didn't pray well enough. Jail twenty-two barbers for providing "Titanic" haircuts (à la Leonardo DiCaprio) because hair on your forehead interferes with your ability to say your prayers.

I had a taste of life with the Taliban myself during an unexpected stay in their foreign compound on the outskirts of Kandahar. Because my declared interest in traveling to Afghanistan was to visit the Institute of Orthopaedics, Zalmai Mojadidi had arranged for me to stay in the guesthouse of a non-government organization his Guardians organization worked for. But since I was visiting when the UN placed sanctions on the Taliban in January 2001, the staff of the guesthouse had been evacuated to Islamabad, and I needed to find new lodgings. I found shelter with another NGO but knew my presence was a source of concern for them. The atmosphere was exceptionally tense, and the last thing those who stayed in Kandahar wanted was a journalist prowling around. Soon after I left the Institute of Orthopaedics, I knew trouble was afoot. Mojadidi said the hotel had refused me a room because I was a foreigner. We tried an Afghan guesthouse. They said I couldn't stay there because I was a woman. It was midafternoon, the sun was starting to set. I had an ominous feeling that the various proprietors had been told not to take me in, so I went as quickly as I could to the Red Cross Compound and asked the director for advice. He said, "Get over to the United Nations Compound immediately and stay in their guesthouse. There's lots of room since almost everyone's been evacuated for fear of reprisals during the sanctions."

In great haste, as it was now four o'clock and the streets were starting to empty, I drove to the UN compound and begged shelter. Leslie Oqvist, the regional coordinator for the UN in Kandahar, refused me, explaining that journalists were not allowed shelter in the compound. I tried to explain that I felt less like a journalist at this moment and more like a citizen in trouble. My protestations were to no avail. I was seen to the door. Five minutes later, a Taliban pickup truck pulled up next to the vehicle I was in, and the driver told Mojadidi to follow them to the Taliban Foreign Compound. We sped through the now dark streets of Kandahar and out of town to the appointed compound. It wasn't hard to spot. Barbed-wire fences and searchlights surrounded the buildings clustered together; to this "foreign guest" it looked like a concentration camp. Once close to the buildings, I realized there was yet another fence, a tall metal barrier surrounding the buildings.

Mojadidi kept translating the words of the men in the pickup truck. "We're taking you here for your own safety," they said over and over again. It started to sound more like the script of a B-grade Hollywood movie about captives.

Inside, to my great surprise, I saw another woman. Esther Oxford, a freelance journalist, was working on a story for the *Sunday Times* in Britain. We'd met earlier in the week and compared notes about the annoyance and anxiety of trying to get information in a place where one group constantly lies and everyone else is too afraid to speak. She called out to me, "You're under house arrest. I've been here for three days and they won't let me go." The gate guard ushered me past Esther and showed me to a room where I would be their "guest." The room had a lock on the outside of the door. It was not an encouraging sign.

I joined Esther outside and together we watched through the window while the guard rifled through my backpack. She told me that she had also begged shelter from Mr. Oqvist at the United Nations compound and had been refused. The night was cool; the rock-strewn desert floor we were sitting on was as uninviting as the guards; and it struck me as odd that the stars were twinkling in the sky, just as they would be if I was at home in the safety of my own backyard on a clear, cold night.

Soon enough Esther and I were summoned to the house. Esther gave me a quick rundown about what would happen next, that dinner would be served and that we would be joined by a Taliban chieftain at the table. Sure enough, platters of rice were brought to a long narrow table. In defiance we'd left our chadors behind in our rooms and had each agreed to try to get more information from the scowling man who sat down with us. We didn't get far. Dinner was a one-way conversation, a speech about his interpretation of Islam and the West. We were the infidels; he was the holy man. I selected silence for the rest of the meal.

Afterwards we were dismissed to rest and reminded again that we were there for our own safety. It was a long night. Lying on a hard board with my notebooks stuffed into my clothes, I watched the searchlight sweep by the window every two or three minutes and listened to the footsteps outside my locked door, wondering if Esther was doing the same in the room she'd been assigned in another part of the building. Dawn finally came and with it an announcement that I come back to the main room where I found hot green tea and not-so-hot naan bread for breakfast. Esther and I went back outside to the desert patio and pondered the next steps in our sojourn. One of the guards, whom Esther called her minder, told her she would leave that day for another city and that he would accompany her "for your own safety." Another told me that Mojadidi would collect me mid-morning and that together we would leave the country. I wrapped up in my chador and was heading to the gate to wait for Mojadidi when the scowling man from dinner the night before reappeared and told me to pay him $30 U.S. I was astonished but decided it was a cheap ticket out; however, I only had $20 bills. I offered him $40 and thought I would lose the change, but to my surprise, he reached into his pocket and returned a $10 bill. I decided that asking for a receipt might be pushing my luck, and I returned to the gate to wait in hope for my Danny DeVito rescuer. Shortly afterwards, he arrived and we left for a few more interviews before hitting the road back to Pakistan.

Things were not getting better in Afghanistan. The tragedy of the Taliban taking over a country was not about wearing a burqa, although that issue was the flashpoint for worldwide attention. It was about refusing education to girls and denying jobs to women and closing hospitals and health clinics. In the winter of 2001, Afghanistan was teetering on the edge of calamity.

When I bid farewell to the women I met during that voyage, their canny analysis and witty descriptions about their lives under the Taliban gave way to darker realities. With trepidation and in barely audible whispers, they implored me to take their story to the world outside, to ask the women in the world to help them. They said, "Get our schools open, get us back to work, or get us out of here."

Chapter 7

HUMAN RIGHTS, HUMAN WRONGS

The "holy warriors" running Afghanistan had no theological qualms about violating the women and girls they kept behind purdah walls. Rape, abduction and forced marriages had been part of life and death under the mujahideen, but the Taliban sanctioned the brutalization of women and girls. Although the women whispered about cases of egregious abuse, it wasn't until the Taliban were chased from Kabul that those stories were documented by organizations such as Human Rights Watch. Women and girls were sexual prizes to the Taliban warriors, grabbed as the spoils of war and used as concubines, sold as sex slaves to wealthy Arabs, with the profits being used

125

to feed the war machine. Violence invariably went unreported because the Taliban's methods for dealing with malcontents was to kill them. Moreover, the women and girls couldn't even report their abuse to family members because of the age-old issue of "honor." If a woman is defiled, she has dishonored the family and must be killed. One way or another, females in Afghanistan knew that suffering in silence was their only choice.

During the five-year rule of the Taliban, the banning of health care for women created the highest maternity mortality rate in the world. Afghan women have a one-in-twelve chance of dying in childbirth; one-in-four that their children will die before the age of five. Those who survive past age five still face huge difficulties.

By the time the world lifted the veil on Afghanistan in the fall of 2001, UNICEF had identified one million children in dire need and 100,000 who would die before winter set in if they didn't receive immediate help. A measles epidemic was raging, polio was widespread, and the children were suffering from malnutrition and exposure. They were succumbing to common infections like colds simply because of their weakened immune systems.

While all of the children of Afghanistan are in desperate need of help, the plight of the girl child is particularly severe. Like other girls in the developing world, she's fed last and least. But in Afghanistan, the threat to the health of girls and their mothers was unparalleled.

The human rights of half a billion women and girls in the world today are being abrogated by governments that are never brought to account. And yet all of those governments, including Afghanistan, have signed treaties at the United Nations that clearly include health care as a human right. The treatment of women and girls in Afghanistan was therefore in contravention of the Declaration of Human Rights; the International Covenant on Economic, Social, and Cultural Rights; the Convention on the Elimination of All Forms of

Discrimination Against Women; and the Convention on the Rights of the Child. Documenting the human-rights abuses during the Taliban regime was a confounding task, because access to Afghanistan was difficult if not impossible and there was no constitution, rule of law or independent judiciary.

Although organizations such as UNICEF and Dr. Sima Samar's Shuhada Clinic had reported a steady deterioration of health during the dark days of the Taliban, only one formal study was done—by an organization called Physicians for Human Rights (PHR). This non-government organization mobilizes health professionals and enlists support from the general public to protect and promote human rights. PHR's belief is that human rights are an essential precondition for health and well-being. With that in mind, they felt the denial of health rights to Afghan women and girls had to be recorded. But getting into the country to collect the necessary data required a daring and creative plan.

During the first three months of 1998 PHR dispatched investigators to Kabul; the risk to both researchers and participants was considerable, but reliable data was needed. The researchers conducted a three-part study that included a health and human-rights survey of 160 Afghan women; detailed case histories of forty Afghan women; and interviews with twelve humanitarian assistance providers, health personnel and other experts. The domains of inquiry for each study component included Afghan women's physical-health status and access to health care, mental-health status, war-related trauma and land-mine exposure, experiences of abuse by Taliban officials, and attitudes toward women's human rights. The results were published in a report called *The Taliban's War on Women: A Health and Human Rights Crisis in Afghanistan*.

The findings were stunning. Not only was the health and well-being of women and girls declining drastically, but the repercussions for the next generation were already evident.

In the survey of 160 Afghan women, 71 percent of the participants reported a decline in their physical health between 1996, when the Taliban regime began, and 1998, when the survey was conducted. The majority of respondents (77 percent) reported poor access to health-care services in Kabul during the past year of residence there, and 20 percent reported no access. Both the access to care and the quality of health-care services in Kabul were deemed much worse over the past year compared with two years prior by a majority of the participants (62 percent and 58 percent respectively). In addition 53 percent of women described occasions in which they were seriously ill and unable to seek medical care. The women consistently described high levels of poor health, with multiple specific symptoms. An Afghan physician described declining nutrition in children, an increasing rate of tuberculosis and a high prevalence of other infectious diseases among women and children.

The Physicians for Human Rights study also surveyed the hospitals available to women and girls and found that they had no clean water, electricity, surgical or medical equipment. They lacked basic medical supplies and equipment such as X-ray machines, suction and oxygen, running water and medications. Female patients said they had received no medical attention; one had not been attended to for ten days. But even these poor facilities were not available to most women and girls. And yet facilities for health services are listed in article 25 of the Universal Declaration of Human Rights, article 12(2)(d) of the International Covenant on Economic, Social and Cultural Rights, article 10(g) and 10(h) and 12(1) of Convention on the Elimination of All Forms of Discrimination Against Women and article 24(1), (2)(b), (2)(e) of the Children's Convention.

In separate semi-structured interviews with forty Afghan women, they explored access to health-care services. Of the forty women interviewed, 87 percent reported a decrease in

Sally with Sima Samar and her daughter, Tamanna, near Quetta, 1997.

Fatima Gailani. "A woman with a scarf is not more holy than a woman without a scarf," 1997.

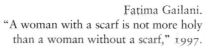

Pharmacist Mina Ali had to stay home and wear a burqa, 1997.

All photos by Sally Armstrong unless otherwise noted.

Custom dictates that Dr. Sima show a patient's relatives what she removed during the surgery, 1997.

So proud of her baby,
so afraid to show her face, 1997.

Dr. Sima scrubs for surgery, March 1997.

Farahnaz Mehdiz (left), a civil engineer, and Fatana Osman, a psychiatrist, were forbidden to work, 1997.

Dr. Sima and her sister-in-law, Nasreen, at the Shuhada Clinic, 1997.

Lunch time with (from left to right) Rauf, Sima, Tamanna, Sally and
Sima's mother, Kurshid, January 2000.

Mother and daughter, 2000.

Sick, scared and lost
while bombs fell in 2001.

Sima at the University of Toronto with Sally. December 2001.
(*W4WAfghanistan, Guelph Chapter*)

The only time I had to wear a burqa:
with Noor Mhammad and Mhammad Naim in Kabul, 2002.

Broken windows, crowded classrooms and a chance to learn.
The children are back in school, 2002.

A bakery in Kandahar, next to
the Red Mosque, February 2002.
(Thorne Anderson)

"Now we can show our faces."
Left to right back row: Sima Shahnawaz, Rozia Kamand, Frozan
Mahram and Torpeky Kohdamany.
Front row: Sharifa Reza Mohseny and Zarghona Sakhy.
Kandahar, 2002.

Minister of Women's Affairs Sima Samar
holds a meeting in her new office, February 2002.

Home again in Kabul,
Hamida Omid is principal of
the Women's High School.

Back to school:
They sit three to a desk in a cold schoolroom but are happy to be there.

their access to health services. The reasons given included: no chaperone available (27 percent), restrictions on women's mobility (36 percent), hospital policy that refused to provide care to women (21 percent), no female doctor available (48 percent), not owning a burqa so unable to leave home (6 percent) and economics (61 percent).

The investigators reported that the interference with the right to health care was not limited to hospitals. At medical facilities outside the hospitals—clinics and midwife stations, for example—Taliban guards were always present and intervened at will on behalf of the Department for the Propagation of Virtue and Suppression of Vice. Nurses and other staff feared being beaten when not covered completely, women were afraid to leave their homes to seek care, male physicians feared examining a woman even when she was accompanied by a brother, husband or son, because they were forbidden to touch the women. One dentist described his fear of examining a woman's teeth because she would have to lift her burqa from her face and if he was caught they would both be beaten and jailed. Another woman was mourning the death of her daughter who had suffered stomach pains for days but could not be taken out because the woman didn't own a burqa.

And although many international organizations regarded the burqa as a culturally sensitive issue and not the business of outsiders, the PHR researchers found that the burqa itself may contribute to health problems. A female pediatrician they interviewed noted, "My activities are restricted. Walking with the burqa is difficult; it has so many health hazards. You can't see well and there is a risk of falling or getting hit by a car. Also for the women with asthma or hypertension, wearing a burqa is very unhealthy."

The Taliban insist that women themselves consented to the edicts, that the population was showing its piety by living according to Islam. But the research revealed that the consent was coerced, that many women hated being totally covered by a burqa and resented how they were denied employment, education and health care. They consented only because they feared for their lives.

Gender inequality is evident at every stage of an Afghan girl's life, but when the data around her access to health services is considered, her inequality can only be described as gender apartheid. The so-called religious edicts make women unjustly unequal to men to the point that they interfere with their health and, in some cases, with their right to life. For example, a health report from Dr. Samar's Shuhada clinic highlights rules that lead directly to sexual violence:

If a girl is raped by somebody she will be killed. The Taliban want the eyewitness [reports] of adult Muslim, mentally healthy males to condemn the man who raped the girl. Naturally, it is very difficult to find these witnesses for a rape case. To kill the girl because of the pregnancy after she had been raped, they do not ask eyewitnesses because she already is the proof. She cannot have a legal abortion. She will have an unhygienic abortion and most probably she will die from the abortion. If she is very lucky, her family will be in solidarity with her and move to another town or village to escape the honor killing. But in most cases, the family will kill her to save their honor, or the Taliban will kill her in the public hall of honor. They'll stone her to death or hang her, as they did recently.

There is no justice and law to protect her and no place where she can go and be safe. Sometimes the mother will be killed with the daughter.

Samar reports that before the Taliban took power, family planning was available. It was only after the arrival of the

Taliban that family planning was considered an un-Islamic action. Although family planning is stated as a required human right in articles 12(1) and 14(b) of the Women's Convention, it was banned by the Taliban (except in a very few cases where the facilities were available and the women could get permission from their husbands). Samar is concerned about the young generation. "Most of them have four or five children by the age of twenty. It's usual that the girl is pregnant while she's still feeding the last born. That's why most of these girls are suffering from anemia and osteomalacia and it's why the mother and child mortality and morbidity rate in Afghanistan is the highest in the world."

Another doctor reported to the Physicians for Human Rights researchers that the burqa causes eye problems and poor vision, poor hearing, skin rash, headaches, increased cardiac problems and asthma, itching of the scalp, alopecia (hair loss) and depression. Dr. Samar adds that by wearing a burqa, women are deprived of vitamin D from sunshine. That, along with psychological harm, had created epidemic levels of osteomalacia and depression among the women of Afghanistan.

Samar also says the lack of health education facilities and the corresponding lack of knowledge about body functions has created additional problems. "Since all the girls' schools have been closed, there is no education facility in general but, in particular, no biology lesson. The girls cannot even see their friends and talk to each other about the changes in their bodies." She reports that most mothers are not educated and don't know anything about their own bodies to tell their daughters. And in any case, the culture does not allow anyone to speak about the female body. "The majority of the girls who reach puberty and have their first menses are shocked and do not know what is happening to their body. So they try to hide and, not surprisingly, some of them become depressed." Most girls are married very young, soon after their twelfth birthday. They are denied the information promised to them in the Children's Convention and are counted as property by their husbands, which also contravenes the treaties Afghanistan has signed.

Dr. Samar reports that trichomoniasis (vaginal infection), candidiasis (yeast-like parasitic fungus) and pelvic infection are common among the young women. "They have no information about their bodies and think that the blood coming from their vagina is dirty blood, so they usually try to hide their menses from the other members of the family." She reports they use dirty, old cloths as menstruation napkins because they haven't any money to buy soap to wash them and they cannot dry the cloths in the sun since such evidence of being female must not be seen by anyone. When they get sick they can't even discuss the reasons for their disease with a doctor because they can only go to the doctor with a male relative and they cannot talk about menses in front of their male relatives.

The added consequences of living under a government that thumbs its nose at its human-rights obligations is the rising incidence of mental and neurological disease. Participants in the survey done by the Physicians for Human Rights had extraordinarily high levels of mental stress and depression. Eighty-one percent reported a decline in their mental condition. A large number of respondents (42 percent) met the diagnostic criteria for post-traumatic stress disorder and major depression (97 percent), and also demonstrated significant symptoms of anxiety (86 percent). Twenty-one percent indicated they had suicidal thoughts "extremely often" or "quite often." It is clear from the interviews done with Afghan women that the general climate of cruelty, abuse and tyranny that characterized Taliban rule has had a profound affect on women's mental health. Ninety-five percent of the women interviewed described a decline in their mental health during the last two years.

Researcher Zohra Rasekh examined the data around twenty-one adolescent girls who were interviewed as part of the larger group to determine the effects of health-care denial on young girls. Two had suffered serious injuries from land-mines resulting in loss of limbs. Neither had received rehabili-tation for their injuries. All of the adolescents interviewed described feelings of anxiety, overwhelming sadness, fear about the future and hopelessness. Four adolescents described frequent nightmares, and two explicitly talked about their wish to end their lives. One sixteen-year-old girl interviewed in Kabul said, "Sometimes I think suicide may be a way out of this horrible life, but I feel sympathy for my mother since I am all she has in this world."

Samar echoed the Physicians for Human Rights study with her own calculations of the incidence of depression among girls between the ages of ten and twenty. She reported varying levels of depression in all of her patients and says the reasons are many. Isolation was a big factor: the girls couldn't go to school or see their friends. This was especially difficult for girls who had been to school before. The ban on entertainment meant there was no television, no magazines, no music, no pictures, no news about the world. The poor economy—especially in the big cities where, prior to the Taliban takeover, parents were working and the children were going to school—has meant going to bed hungry. That, coupled with the lack of hope about their situation, induces depression.

The formula at work here was awesomely effective in keeping women in medical purdah. The socially constructed role of women in Afghanistan created a victim-based system that withdrew health services on the one hand and blamed the victim for poor health on the other. Similarly, the socio-historical and religious aspects of a woman's life in Afghanistan contributed to making this treatment of women seem natural and accepted. Add the punitive power of the Taliban to the mix and it becomes obvious that the ideology was highly resistant to change.

The human-rights documents that are international law were worthless to the women and girls of Afghanistan, and the world seemed powerless to even keep them alive under Taliban control, much less gain access to health services for them. There was a presumption that a rogue government such as the Taliban was not obliged to observe the treaties the country signed. The Physicians for Human Rights report states, "Under international law, the Taliban is responsible for adherence to human-rights laws Afghanistan has ratified, notwithstanding the fact that its leadership does not recognize the validity of these to the extent that they depart from the Taliban's particular interpretation of Shari'a." Moreover, they argued that the fact that the Taliban did not possess all of the attributes of a functioning and recognized government did not relieve it of accountability for the human-rights violations it committed.

Prior to the Taliban takeover, Afghanistan had become party to many human-rights treaties. It was the first country to accede to the Convention on the Political Rights of Women in 1966. It also acceded to the International Covenant on Civil and Political Rights and the International Covenant on Economic, Social and Cultural Rights in 1983 without reservation. And it signed, although did not ratify, the Convention on the Elimination of All Forms of Discrimination Against Women in 1980. The committee that monitors the Women's Convention specifically stated at the thirteenth session in 1994 that Shari'a law itself gave equality to women, but the problem that had to be overcome was that of interpretation. Afghanistan also signed the Children's Convention in 1994 but made a general reservation on all provisions of the convention that are incompatible with Shari'a law and local legislation.

Freedom of religion allows for specific interpretations of, and reservations under, international law. But it doesn't permit the Taliban to take measures that directly contravene the object and purpose of treaties under which it has assumed obligations, nor to decline to uphold universally recognized principles of non-discrimination in the name of Shari'a. For example, article 6 in the International Covenant on Civil and Political Rights specifies the right to life, but the Taliban denied access to life-saving health care. Article 7 prohibits torture or cruel, inhuman or degrading treatment, yet the Taliban not only called for stoning a woman to death as a punishment but stated that the stones thrown must not be so large as to kill her quickly. Article 16 recognizes the right of everyone to be recognized as a person before the law, but in Afghanistan during the Taliban rule, girls and woman had no rights. Article 18 establishes freedom of thought, conscience and religion, a moot point in the case of Afghan women and girls. Moreover, those rights that the Taliban denied to women and girls are called "non-derogable rights," which means they cannot be suspended even during times of war, according to the UN treaties that the government of Afghanistan signed.

Those treaties uphold the rights of women and girls to bodily integrity, information, education, association, freedom of movement and health care. The Taliban therefore committed gross violations of human rights, in both their imposition of severe restrictions on women and girls' activities and movement and their harsh punishment for failure to adhere to these restrictions. "Even though the Taliban is not an officially recognized government of Afghanistan, it is still accountable for the human-rights violations it has perpetrated against Afghan women," reports Physicians for Human Rights.

The World Health Organization defines health as "a state of complete physical, mental, and social well-being and not merely the absence of disease or infirmity." Therefore health care requires protection and promotion of human rights. The Taliban restrictions on women and girls obviously denied those rights. The research done by the Physicians for Human Rights demonstrates that the violations of these rights of women and

girls have had deleterious mental- and physical-health consequences. The experiences and concerns of Afghan women and
girls documented in these studies illustrate that the promotion
of their health is inextricably linked to the protection of their
human rights. And they demonstrate that the Taliban in
Afghanistan were in contravention of the Declaration of
Human Rights, as well as all the other treaties they signed, by
denying girls and women health care and in promoting laws
that damage their health. The treatment of Afghan women
and girls makes it obvious that denial of health care, which is
influenced by cultural and ideological factors, such as the
subordination of women and girls and the systemic inequalities
they experience, was illegal as well as catastrophic for future
generations. Samar reports, "My personal experience as a
female medical doctor working in and out of Afghanistan since
1982 shows that the health situation of the girls was getting
worse and worse." She closes her report with a commentary
from Afghan feminist author Nawal El Saadawi:

> All children who are born healthy and normal feel that they
> are complete human beings. This, however, is not so for the
> female child. From the moment she is born and even before
> she learns to pronounce words, the way people look at her,
> the expression in their eyes, and their glances somehow
> indicate that she was born "incomplete" or "with some-
> thing missing." From the day of her birth to the moment of
> death, a question will continue to haunt her: "Why?" Why
> is it that preference is given to her brother, despite the fact
> that they are the same, or that she may even be superior to
> him in many ways, or at least in some aspects?
>
> The first aggression experienced by the female child in
> society is the feeling that people do not welcome her
> coming into the world. In some families, and especially in
> rural areas, this "coldness" may go even further and

become an atmosphere of depression and sadness, or even lead to the punishment of the mother with insults or blows or even divorce.

But there's another sad fact reported, not by poets like Saadawi, but rather by researchers who discovered some hard truths about the Taliban and were rebuked for bringing them to light. Zohra Rasekh, a senior health researcher, was sponsored by PHR to conduct its study in Afghanistan; she was also one of the authors of the report. She returned to the region from Washington in the winter of 2000 with another team of researchers from Physicians for Human Rights to interview people who'd come from Shamali, an area north of Kabul, and discovered a new kind of horror being perpetrated by the men who called themselves holy warriors. She spent two months in the region with six research assistants and talked to 300 men and 300 women. The report they filed contained ample evidence that the Taliban had burned villages, killed the men and raped the women as they roamed from province to province while they took over most of the country. Everyone in Afghanistan knew about women being kidnapped and sold as brides to wealthy Arabs—and taken as sexual slaves by Taliban warriors. Everyone knew the Taliban were raping women when they invaded villages. But until Rasekh's report, no one had recorded data from eyewitnesses.

Rasekh heard many distressing cases during her survey. One of them came from a young mother, Jamila, with five young children, ages nine months to seven years. Jamila wept as she recalled what happened:

It was around noon. My husband, a poor farmer, was getting ready to go to the field, my children were playing outside and I was cooking lunch. I saw my husband going onto the roof. He came down quickly and said, "They are

getting close to our village. They will attack us." I knew
he was talking about the Taliban. The militia had attacked
and burned a village nearby the day before. Pacing up and
down, he kept saying, "They are not going to hurt us.
They are Muslim. We are poor farmers." Five minutes
later, we heard a loud explosion and gunfire outside our
qala [mud house]. Then four armed men with long black
beards, dark outfits and black turbans, carrying butcher
knives and Kalashnikovs, barged into our backyard.

My husband was terrified. He held my hand tightly and
told the men not to hurt him. They pointed a knife at his
face and told him to come outside with them. My
husband kept begging them to let him go: "I have four
young children and my wife is eight months pregnant.
Please don't hurt us." The armed men pushed him down
on the ground, covered his eyes with cloth and tied his
hands behind his back, then dragged him out of the *qala*.

My children were screaming. All of a sudden, I felt a
severe pain in my back. I lay down on the floor. Two
Taliban fighters came into the room and yelled, "Leave or
you'll be burned together with your home." I told them
that I couldn't get up. They saw I was in labor and left.

Hours later, I opened my eyes and saw my baby
between my legs. I wrapped the baby in my scarf. My
other children were hiding behind the *rakhte-khwab*
[comforters and pillows] in the corner, all asleep. I went to
the backyard and saw sixteen bodies in the garden. I
recognized the bodies of my husband and his two brothers; the rest were our male relatives and neighbors. I
screamed and ran to the roof; I wanted to jump off and
kill myself. I screamed, "Come and kill us, too. You killed
my children's father; come and kill us all." I really didn't
want to live without the father of my children. But my
baby's cry persuaded me not to jump.

My brother, who lives in another village, heard about the attack and came to save us. The next day we fled to Kabul, but because Kabul was controlled by Taliban, we escaped to Pakistan. This is where we live now, without shelter or enough food. My children have little to eat and they freeze at nights under this makeshift tent. In the evenings, I go from tent to tent to beg for bread.

Rasekh was soundly rebuked by Nora Niland, the gender specialist for the United Nations in Islamabad, who asked her how she dared to go into Afghanistan and make the Taliban look like monsters.

However, just one month later, UN rapporteur Kamal Hossain provided testimony to the UN Commission on Human Rights about ethnic Hazara and Tajik women being rounded up in trucks and taken from the regions of Mazar-e-Sharif, Pol-e-Khomri and Shamali to neighboring Pakistan and the Taliban stronghold of Kandahar. "Many suspect that women and girls end up forced into prostitution," his report said. "Women have been killed and maimed trying to escape from these trucks." His report also gave evidence that non-Afghans, including Arabs and Pakistanis who were fighting alongside the Taliban, were also involved in the rights violations against women and ethnic minorities.

Physicians for Human Rights refused to publish Rasekh's report, claiming it was biased and not properly randomized. Niland's rebuke led Rasekh to believe that the UN and some NGOs had pressured Physicians for Human Rights to stop the publication of the facts. She was furious and tried to get the data back and publish it herself. "The data about women being raped and abused was valuable evidence," said Rasekh. "Moreover, apart from my research, the people had complained to me that there was no assistance for them. The food wasn't reaching them. They didn't have shelter. There was no access to health care. My report asked where this assistance was going and who was checking the non-government organization projects." Instead, she was told by PHR not to talk about it. There was no analysis done on her work; it was simply filed away.

It wasn't the first time people had questioned the way the United Nations was managing the Taliban. "The UN knew what was going on and were like a de facto government in Afghanistan," says Rasekh. "I felt frustrated, isolated. Many in the NGO community saw me as the enemy. They didn't want the Taliban exposed as it would affect the work they were doing." It's true the Taliban threatened to throw out any NGOs who didn't go along with their so-called cultural rules for women. In the face of gendered help, as opposed to no help, most NGOs felt they should try to broker some sort of peace with the Taliban so they could get assistance to as many people as possible. But it was a bitter pill for those who saw the human rights of half the population threatened every single day. For Rasekh, the pill she had to swallow was made slightly less bitter when the Taliban were chased out of the country and the reports she had tried to file were made public by the Afghan people themselves—in news reports that followed the ousting of the Taliban, as well as by Human Rights Watch in New York. It was the abrogating of human rights that attracted people like Rasekh there in the first place. The righting of those wrongs kept her and many other women on the case until the rest of the world found out the truth.

Chapter 8

IS ANYONE LISTENING?

While the women of Afghanistan turned into virtual pillars of salt during the five long years they were imprisoned by the Taliban, most of the world went about business as usual. But many women's groups dedicated themselves to strategic planning to help these oppressed women. Some, like the members of the Revolutionary Association of the Women of Afghanistan (RAWA), wrapped themselves in burqas, concealed cameras and notebooks under their garments and went underground in Afghanistan. They managed to obtain video evidence of the suffocating lives of women and girls, as well as the execution of a woman in Kabul's soccer stadium. Others, like the

141

Feminist Majority in the United States, created a brilliant lobby campaign to shut down powerful corporations in the West that were supporting the Taliban with business contracts. A women's organization called Shirkat Gah (their leader, Farida Shaheed, is pictured on page 141), in Pakistan, took on the task of educating women about the laws they were living under— and exposing the duplicity of the political-religious leaders. And an association of women from forty countries whose lives were affected by Muslim laws and who had banded together in the 1980s to form an organization called Women Living Under Muslim Laws brought their support and collective experience to the women of Afghanistan. In Canada, women across the country formed groups called Women for Women in Afghanistan (W4WAfghan) and raised money to fund the clandestine schools and health clinics for girls and women in Afghanistan and income-generating projects for Afghan women in refugee camps.

From the United States to Australia, from Canada to Pakistan, from the women in Kabul to those in the sprawling Afghan diaspora and Muslim communities throughout the world, the group's initiatives to expose the suffering of 11.5 million women were brave, determined and downright daring. Their goals were unequivocal. Shut down the Taliban or force them to let the women go back to work and the girls go back to school. In the meantime, fund the clandestine schools and health clinics in the country. Provide help for women in the refugee camps. Support Afghan women leaders who were at the front line facing the foe. And censure those who would profit from these calamities.

Canada

When I left the Afghan women after my first voyage to the region in 1997, they begged me to ask Canadian women to speak for them. They said, "We no longer have a voice; we need other women to become our voice." And in astonishing numbers, that's what women in Canada—from coast to coast to coast—did.

It started with the response to a 1997 article I wrote for *Homemaker's* magazine about the plight of the women I had met. Within days of publication, the fax machine was humming, the e-mails were pouring in from cyberspace, and big gray mailbags were being dragged into the Toronto editorial office. Throughout that late spring and summer, more than 9,000 letters arrived from women all across Canada, demanding something be done about the ghastly conditions of the women in Afghanistan. The letters were delivered to Canada's foreign minister at the time, the Honorable Lloyd Axworthy. In September he addressed the General Assembly of the United Nations. "Canadian women are appalled at the treatment of their sisters in Afghanistan and have started a letter-writing campaign," he said. "I will be delivering their letters to the secretary general, which call on him to take the lead in exposing the gross human-rights violations of the women of Afghanistan as unacceptable in the eyes of the world's citizens."

Axworthy then contacted the magazine's editorial office, seeking to arrange for Dr. Sima Samar, who'd been profiled in the article, to attend a round-table consultation in Ottawa, the nation's capital. He wanted her to assist in discussing a strategy for dealing with the Taliban and taking further action on women's rights in Afghanistan. Dr. Samar came to Canada in November 1997 and talked to the gathering. "Some people talk about this terrible oppression as though women accept it. That's not true. We aren't from another planet. We don't agree with that oppression at all."

At the round table she urged Canada to put pressure on the Taliban to allow the girls to go back to school and the women to return to work. "Canada is a country that can make alliances with countries such as the United States and countries supporting the Taliban such as Pakistan and Saudi Arabia," she said. "Canadian people care a lot about human rights. Your government can pressure the Taliban to change their policies toward women."

When asked what she wanted Canadian women to do, she replied, "We need solidarity and sisterhood. We want you to speak for us because we don't have a voice in our country right now. . . . So far, the UN is being very passive toward the women of Afghanistan. We want them to take more action. We're part of the female global body. If we are hurt, other women are hurt." She went on to praise the Canadians' effort: "I am probably quoted in one newspaper or magazine every month. I have never had a reaction like the one from Canadian women, who have been exceptional in their response to our problem. I know the time and effort it takes to compose and send a letter of protest. It says a lot about Canadian women that you take time from your busy lives to care about other women. You have made us feel that we are not alone."

The Canadian women she referred to were busy launching Women for Women in Afghanistan groups all across the country. Janice Eisenhower and her W4WAfghan group in Calgary, Alberta, published a newsletter to keep the groups in contact with one another, and established a Web page to provide international updates.

Seven women met in Toronto in November 1999 to discuss the need to take the campaign to another level, and they met with Foreign Affairs Minister Lloyd Axworthy a month later. He made several suggestions, including forming a national coalition, creating a resolution for the International Status of Women meeting being held in New York in February 2000, creating an awareness-building campaign, lobbying the American government to get the women on the same agenda as Osama bin Laden, and holding a national conference.

Axworthy promised that if those things were accomplished, he would take the issue to the Security Council when Canada's representative became president of the council on April 1, 2000.

The Canadian Coalition in Support of Afghan Women was established in February 2000. More than eighty-six organizations and individuals were contacted. A national conference was planned for June in Toronto. The Body Shop raised the awareness level by including the women of Afghanistan in their Stop Violence Against Women, 2000 campaign. Human-rights lawyer Marilou McPhedran wrote the resolution to be presented at the International Status of Women meeting. It said: "Be it resolved that Canada must lead the UN Security Council in redressing the oppression of women and girls under the Taliban regime in Afghanistan and other countries where women suffer from grievous and systemic violations of women's human rights, such as denial of personal autonomy, freedom of movement, right of assembly, access to employment opportunities and basic services such as education and health care."

More than sixty women's non-government organizations took the resolution to the Canadian Consultation of the Feminist Alliance for International Action held February 11–14, 2000. The resolution was passed at that meeting and carried to the Status of Women meeting in New York. And coalition members teamed with the largest women's organization in the U.S., the Feminist Majority, to press the American government to include the plight of Afghan women on the same agenda as the Osama bin Laden file.

Minister Axworthy kept his word. On April 7 his inaugural address, marking Canada's presidency of the Security Council at the United Nations, focused on the women and girls of Afghanistan. He began by welcoming Angela King, assistant secretary-general and advisor on gender issues and the advancement of women to the Security Council. "Her presence here today underlines one of the darkest aspects of the conflict in that desperate country—the appalling violation of the rights of women and girls, in particular under the Taliban," he said. "All aspects of this conflict are reprehensible. But some stand out more than others. Perhaps the most disturbing is the Taliban's systemic pattern of violation of the human rights of half the population—women and girls—a violation that the Taliban misrepresent as having a religious foundation."

The national conference of the Canadian Coalition in Support of Afghan Women was held at York University in Toronto on June 10, 2000. It attracted women from across Canada. Michele Landsberg, a well known human rights activist and *Toronto Star* columnist, had been following the plight of Afghan women and alerted her readers to the conference. Within days of the column being published, the event reached capacity registration. Then minister of international co-operation, Maria Minna, addressed the three hundred registrants, and the gathering created action plans to apply pressure on governments that supported the Taliban, to promote awareness in Canada and around the world, and to embarrass the Taliban internationally.

The United States

On December 10, 1998, Hillary Rodham Clinton marked the fiftieth anniversary of the Declaration of Human Rights with a speech about the women of Afghanistan. "The most egregious and systematic trampling of human rights of any person is taking place in Afghanistan today against women," she said. "We cannot allow these terrible crimes against women and girls—and truly against all of humanity—to continue with impunity. We must all make it unmistakably clear that this terrible suffering inflicted on the women and girls of Afghanistan is not cultural, it is criminal. And we must do everything in our power to stop it."

The Feminist Majority had been working on the case for two years when the former First Lady spoke out. They had mobilized over 225 women's-rights and human-rights groups to join their Campaign to Stop Gender Apartheid and censure the Taliban, as well as Pakistan and Saudi Arabia for supporting the regime.

It was commonly believed, in 1996, that the Taliban would soon be granted recognition as the official government of Afghanistan by the United States and the United Nations. The Feminist Majority campaign dramatically increased visibility for the women of Afghanistan and kept the pressure on the UN and the U.S. government to deny the Taliban recognition. Feminist Majority Foundation (FMF) President Eleanor Smeal and campaign chair Mavis Leno appeared on all the major news shows, and after a letter from Leno appeared in the "Dear Abby" column, over 15,000 people called to request "Action Packets" from the Feminist Majority.

By framing the issue as gender apartheid—and popularizing the wearing of swatches of the burqa mesh fabric as a symbol of remembrance for Afghan women—the FMF tried to bring the plight of the Afghan women to center stage in the U.S. and the world. They produced two powerful videos, called *Shroud of Silence* and *The Taliban: Prayer of Hate*. In March 1998 President Clinton and UN Secretary-General Kofi Annan announced that the U.S. and the UN respectively would refuse to recognize the Taliban until the human rights of women and girls were restored.

In a bold put-your-money-where-your-mouth-is initiative, chaired by Mavis Leno, the FMF challenged one of the Taliban's potential funders and cut off an expected $100 million a year in Taliban income. For several years, California-based Unocal, a U.S. energy company, was the leader of a consortium to build an oil and gas pipeline from Turkmenistan, through Afghanistan, to Pakistan. The Taliban stood to gain

$100 million a year from the pipeline. The Feminist Majority protested the project in campaigns across the country and during Unocal's annual stockholders' meeting and in demonstrations outside its corporate headquarters. Brilliantly dramatic posters depicting a woman in a burqa with a gas nozzle held to her head were created for the campaign. Unocal canceled the project.

When Telephone Systems International signed a $240 million contract with the Taliban to build a cellular-phone network in Afghanistan, FMF tackled them as well, along with every other company in the U.S. trying to profit from the Taliban, who were known to be paying their suppliers with laundered money from the opium trade. As the Feminist Majority raised awareness of the Taliban, these contracts were usually canceled.

Asked why she got involved in the fight for the women of Afghanistan, Mavis Leno, wife of *Tonight Show* host Jay Leno, told the story of how her father was once buried in a mining accident. "He was dug out and he was fine," she said. "But he told me that while he was buried, the hardest thing was that he had no way of being sure that anyone was looking for him. They could think that maybe he hadn't gone to work that day, or that he was someplace else, not buried. Or maybe they would think, yes, he was buried but he was dead. Maybe they wouldn't look for him.

"That's what came to my mind when I heard about the women in Afghanistan. They don't even know if anybody knows what happened to them. They don't even know if people are trying to save them. And that seemed so terrible to me that I felt I had to be one of the people who was looking for them."

Women Living Under Muslim Laws (WLUML)

While Dr. Samar applauded the women who had banded together to bring worldwide awareness to the issue, she had been working directly with women from forty countries who were affected by the often-misinterpreted laws of Muslim society. The WLUML association began in 1986, when Marienne Heli-Lucas, a Nigerian woman who was based in The Hague, contacted women from Morocco, Egypt, Tunisia, Sri Lanka, Nigeria, Sudan and Pakistan to form a network that could discuss the interpretation of the laws they lived under. They called their association Women Living Under Muslim Laws. Their goal was to stop the isolation of women and to provide linkages and support to all women whose lives were being affected negatively by Muslim laws.

The association was formed in response to punitive interpretations of Muslim law that were harming women during the mid-1980s. Women were being arrested and jailed without trial for discussing issues such as the family code of honor. Women had been stoned to death for alleged sexual impropriety. They were being refused divorces even though the law permitted them. And some women who managed to get a divorce were refused custody of their children.

WLUML highlighted what they saw as two equally important issues. First, the laws that are considered to be Muslim laws vary, sometimes radically, from one cultural context to the other. Second, there are several different legal codes that co-exist in each culture, social and political context. At the very least, each society has a codified legal system and a parallel system of customary laws and practices. Further complicating the matter were subdivisions of the laws into two formal codes in some countries, one being religious, the other civil. And within that context, the customary laws were diverse and often interpreted at the whims of the local mullah or religious leader. These laws were almost always detrimental to women.

The impact of these parallel systems are felt in family and personal matters, which affect women disproportionately and usually in a manner that undermines their rights and autonomy. All too often, the system is presented and internalized as being "Islamic," with many effects on society at large and on women in particular. The different realities for women living under Muslim laws range from being strictly closeted, isolated and voiceless within four walls, subjected to public floggings and condemned to death for presumed adultery and forcibly given in marriage as a child, to situations where women have a far lesser degree of freedom of movement and interaction, are refused the right to work, to participate in public affairs and to exercise control over their own lives.

One of the members of WLUML, Sultana Kamal of Bangladesh, told me she got involved with the organization because she was fed up with working in social services and witnessing the violence and inequities inflicted upon women. "Whenever I questioned the process, the mullah would tell me to be quiet, that I was a woman, not a lawyer and only lawyers understood the law," she said. So she became a lawyer and now works with WLUML. It has links to forty countries, from Fiji to Senegal, and an increasingly powerful voice at the United Nations and in the international law courts.

Until 1991 they trod softly, holding workshops on Koranic interpretations by women and through cross-cultural exchange programs. But with militant fundamentalism on the rise, they became more vocal, more forceful—and in more danger themselves. By 1996, when the Taliban took power, they were the leading voice for women living under Muslim laws.

Pakistan

Farida Shaheed, the Asian coordinator of the association of Women Living Under Muslim Laws in Lahore, Pakistan, won't even use the word fundamentalist. "It suggests a return to cherished fundamentals of Islam, which it certainly is not," she says. "They aren't religious at all. This is political opportunism.

Their strength is in disrupting the political process and using that to blackmail those in political power."

She works at a non-government organization called Shirkat Gah in Pakistan. The goal of this NGO is to educate the women about laws that govern them. Since the vast majority of Afghan women refugees live in northern Pakistan, the work Shirkat Gah does is aimed at empowering the women refugees, as well as women in Pakistan, to understand the law and to protect themselves.

Shaheed says that ultra-religious groups have been used as a vehicle by political parties that are not in power for expressing opposition to the existing regime and challenge the system for political power. The Taliban, for example, were young men who were indoctrinated by a very conservative religious group. They'd never been exposed to the outside world. They generated a tribal response in Afghanistan and in the north of Pakistan when the Soviets left and the mujahideen were fighting each other for power. In the meantime, the attitude of the West, which demonized Muslims as extremists, was fueling the power of the fundamentalists. Shaheed says, "In most Muslim countries coming out of colonialization, there's a tendency to reject things that aren't your own. For people in the Muslim world, the Bosnian war was telling, so was the Gulf War and the ongoing Palestinian situation in the Middle East." It set up a West-versus-East struggle in the minds of the militants.

Shaheed feels the political religious groups gained influence and power because mainstream political parties in Muslim countries have failed to practice democratic rule. But despite the obstacles, she says women were gaining momentum. "There's an unprecedented number of women coming into the workforce at the same time that the political religious groups are saying, 'Stay home.' The programs in literacy and the law being taught by Shirkat Gah were moving women from being victims to renegotiating their spaces. Consider, over 95 percent of the people here have no idea what the law is. They rule their lives according to customs and practices they've had for generations."

Shaheed says the biggest issue is letting women know what their rights are. "Women who aren't literate, aren't educated, believe what they're told and trust what they hear. In a society that oppresses women and has an unequal socializing process, what the women hear sets them up for a lifetime of subjugation." It's that subjugation Shaheed wants to change. For example, she says, "Boys are supposed to dominate and girls are supposed to be docile. There's pressure to get girls married. If a girl is not married, people think she has loose morals. Even when women know their rights, they don't know how to use them. If she tries to rebel and fight for her rights, she subjects herself to beatings. There's no law against wife assault. A lot of what goes on has more to do with culture than fundamentalism.

Shaheed says women living in the village can't distinguish between culture and the law. They aren't independent and they lack confidence, so they don't go to the police. Even for those who would go to the police station, they can't get there on their own, the men won't take them there, and most police stations have a bad reputation for beating women. Although there is a law that says you can include the right to divorce with your marriage, there's a lot of responsibility on the women to make the marriage work, so they won't even ask for the right to divorce, because they think it's a bad omen for the marriage. The police and courts are also part of the problem because, culturally, they think this is a family problem, an issue of honor, dignity and respect.

Shirkat Gah staff teach the laws and statutes to the women, mostly with village groups in Pakistan and to Afghan refugee women in the border cities. Shaheed says, "I'm encouraged by what I'm seeing with young women and, indeed, young men.

The ability for women to have linkages with other women's groups is very important. One woman said the beatings from her husband stopped when her husband realized she had support in the community. The women know they have social workers and lawyers to help them. They've moved from being victims of abuse to helping others who are being abused.

"The law should reflect society's ideal—what should and should not happen in that society," says Shaheed. "The people who legislate law, who wrote the constitution, don't reflect the views of masses of women. The women have not been consulted because of this very traditional form of patriarchy, a feudal system, and mullahs who have enormous power. It means that women have no economic power and very little political power."

The Shirkat Gah program uses human-rights education and consciousness-raising to empower women to make better choices, not to limit themselves. They work with community-based organizations because they can reach more women that way. But Shaheed admits, "It's a very long process and sometimes the women feel they can't do it."

Increasingly, however, the women can handle the challenges that come with changing the status quo. For example, one young girl living in a village was married at the age of four to a boy in the village, also four. They began living together at the age of fourteen. The girl was educated, the boy was not. She had plans for her future and wanted out of the marriage. She couldn't get a divorce simply because they hadn't signed a paper when they were married that said a divorce would be allowed. Shirkat Gah got her a lawyer. The people in the village were angry at first but later realized that the couple had the right to make change for themselves.

"Even in wealthy families, women have to put up with beatings and their men having affairs," says Shaheed. "According to our laws, there is a marriage contract. It gives protection to the woman. But usually she has no idea what that protection is or what those laws are or how to fight back if she does know. She simply has no recourse. We're trying to teach women how to fulfill the marriage contract. The mullahs who often administer the local law and customs are usually uneducated. Often what's being practiced is the culture, and has nothing to do with religion. But to convince the women and keep control over them, the men say it's the law of the Koran. Our studies have shown that it's not the religion, it's the culture and customs that have come down through generations."

For all the rules and regulations, Shaheed says that, at the end of the day, "This is a very hypocritical society. There's a lot of alcohol consumption and girls having boyfriends. In Lahore the girls wear jeans and short skirts, whereas in Quetta, they would be beaten for dressing in what is considered Western fashions. The porn films from Punjab that everyone watches, including the mullahs, are never mentioned. Then the mullahs are hard on the non-government organizations like Shirkat Gah and accuse them of being run by Westernized women who are trespassing on male dominance. When women are independent and know their rights, they won't put up with this nonsense. But that's very threatening to men. The NGOs enrage the Mullahs because the changes that are happening for women are because of the work being done by NGOs."

The women at Shirkat Gah arm themselves by researching the customary practices in the villages and studying both religion and law. For example, the Hudood Ordinances are very discriminatory to women. The Ordinances presume guilt until you are proven innocent, instead of the other way around. "Whatever law exists, if there's an option, it's normally the worst one for women that gets implemented," says Shaheed. For example, the Islamic rules about inheritance say a woman can inherit by law. But women in places like Pakistan and Afghanistan don't inherit because custom says land cannot leave the family. "So they use custom over religion when it suits them, and religion over custom when it suits them. They use justification by way of religion, customs or culture—whatever works at the time."

The women of Shirkat Gah started their programs because they felt they had to do something to create a platform for women's rights and revoke the Islamization of law that Pakistan's General Zia-ul-Haq had brought in during the 1981–1984 period. Shirkat Gah formed women's action forums and in the process, they infuriated the militants who wanted them silenced, sometimes literally. "We would get calls from people claiming they were checking the phones, but we knew they were the government's intelligence people trying to find out what we were doing," says Shaheed. "The most worrisome was when we did a consultancy for the Canadian International Development Agency (CIDA) about the status of women. Their office received a call from someone wanting to know what I was doing in that office and where I lived. The people at CIDA had phoned to warn me."

The women who are trying to change the status of women know very well that the anti-West, post-colonial attitude used by the militants is a modus operandi that embraces the roots of the people and, therefore, the religion and the customs. The more the zealots claim they represent the religion and customs, the more they trumpet an anti-West, anti-colonial spirit, the more likelihood there is of gaining support. "If you focus on making sure the basic needs of the people are served—sanitation, education, health issues—that will automatically undermine the pool from which the political religious parties are getting their support," says Shaheed. The madrassa schools run by the zealots are free and provide food to the students. Her suggestion that governments do the same is well intentioned.

The concerns of human-rights activists like Shaheed, throughout the Taliban regime, was that the support of the women was still being sacrificed for East-West politicking and global ignorance of the women's situation.

RAWA: The Revolutionary Association of the Women of Afghanistan

RAWA was established in Kabul in 1977 as a political-social organization of Afghan women fighting for human rights and social justice in their country. The founders, a group of Afghan women intellectuals, worked under the sagacious leadership of Meena (the women never use their full names and most often use a pseudonym). Meena was assassinated in Quetta, Pakistan, in 1987.

RAWA's objective, then and now, was to involve an increasing number of Afghan women in social and political activities aimed at acquiring women's rights and contributing to the struggle for a democratic and secular government. Despite the repressive political environment, RAWA became involved in widespread activities in different socio-political arenas, including health, education and income generation, as well as political agitation.

A hallmark of RAWA's political activities has been its unrelenting exposure of what its members call the treason and heinous crimes of the fundamentalists. The group launched a bilingual (Persian-Pashto) magazine called *Payme-e-Zan* (women's message) in 1981 and added an English and Urdu translation soon after the Taliban took control. The message was revolution: overthrow the ultra-fundamentalist Taliban, expose their criminal policies and atrocities against the people of Afghanistan in general and stamp out their ultra-male chauvinistic and anti-woman orientation in particular. RAWA went underground in Afghanistan and managed to sneak out eyewitness reports as well as video footage of women being murdered during the Friday "punishments" in Kabul's soccer stadium in 1999. Their film *Behind the Veil* shocked audiences around the world as it exposed the men who called themselves "holy warriors."

The women of RAWA, as well as the members of WLUML, fought back at their peril. Sultana Kamal of Bangladesh has had fire bombs thrown at her house. Farida Shaheed has had her phone tapped. And Sima Samar received so many death threats from the Taliban, she simply replied, "You know where I am. I won't stop what I'm doing."

These are the women who saw the cataclysm coming a decade before the Taliban took power. They raised the alarm but nobody listened. In the early days of Taliban rule, only a few internationally recognized voices joined their protest. One was Carol Bellamy, the executive director of UNICEF in New York, who, in March 1997, predicted a social and economic catastrophe for Afghanistan because of the treatment of its women. Another was Sima Wali, president of Refugee Women In Development (in Washington) who sounded a clarion call to the State Department and women's groups around the world about her native Afghanistan.

Emma Bonino, the commissioner of Humanitarian Affairs for the European Union, also took up the cause. On International Women's Day, March 8, 1998, she launched a campaign called A Flower for the Women of Kabul, to mobilize public opinion around the issue of rights denied to the women of Kabul. "It is an expression of support for them. These women have no hope right now other than us." And another voice came from London, England, where Fatima Gailani—who holds a master's degree in Islamic jurisprudence and is the daughter of Pir Sayyid Ahmad Gailani, the spiritual leader of the Sunni Muslims—lives in exile. Her father is also a descendant of the Prophet, which carries great moral weight. Outraged by the Taliban's interpretation of Islam, Gailani said, "I can prove that any action of the Prophet, his wives—and the Koran—has nothing to do with this. It goes against the Koran, in fact. For example, a woman with a covered head is not more honorable than a woman without a covered head. The Taliban are against Afghan tradition, against Islam. They only continue because presently there is no alternative." With that in mind, she and her father traveled to Rome to meet with the exiled king in March 1997. "My hope was that an Afghan element— the king, the leaders of the tribes, my father—could do something. The Taliban needed aid of every description. They needed money. They'd have responded to pressure."

Pressure was a long time in coming.

Petitions began to circulate around the world on the Internet. One of them circled in cyberspace for four years without ever landing. A student at Brandeis University had started it in good faith. She was reaching out to her fellow students in hopes that, by telling them about what she called the War against Women in Afghanistan, young people would rise up to bring the Taliban down. Instead, it was the university that rose up: the response to the petition was so huge, it crashed the university's system. The student was reprimanded and the petition was canceled. But it was too late. It was already out there in the ether, collecting signatures and urging recipients to sign up and send along the signatures when there were fifty on the page. They were then encouraged to send the petition to everyone on their e-mail list. While no official at the UN ever received this particular petition, it likely did more to raise awareness around the world than any of the other, more authorized ones. While the legitimate protests fulfilled their mandate and expired, this one just circled like space junk, reminding people over and over again that the issue was still there.

Along with the petitions, the women of the world never ceased in their efforts to expose the Taliban's treatment of women. And in the face of sometimes crushing odds and dismissive comments from the United Nations, they pressed on.

Women's groups kept the issue in front of the United Nations. Millions of women marched, signed petitions and raised money. Other than keeping the clandestine schools and health clinics open with their donations and raising awareness, their pleas were largely ignored. After all, to most people, Afghanistan was utterly foreign. Most thought—if they ever thought about the women there at all—that this treatment was something they were conditioned for, a cultural-religious custom that had no effect on the rest of the world.

Then, on a bright, sunlit morning, four planes took off from American airports. It was September 11, 2001.

Chapter 9

SEPTEMBER 11

Suddenly a country most North Americans couldn't have found on a map was front-page news. Suddenly the world saw the women of Afghanistan muffled in their burqas and learned of their restricted lives behind purdah walls. And just as suddenly we saw terrorism being inflicted on Afghanistan—albeit in a different form—as well as in America. The pundits kept repeating, "We'll never be the same."

While I contemplated the horrors in New York and the terror in Afghanistan, I thought those words might have been the single silver lining in the dark cloud that descended that Tuesday morning. We *must* never be the same. We needed to change our view of terrorism as something that happens to *other* people who live in *other* places. We needed to change our view of the lives of those *other* people—those who endure war and poverty and horror on a daily basis.

When we watch conflict on television—the Gulf War, Somalia, Rwanda, Bosnia, Afghanistan—we tend to turn people into "others," into an abstraction. We see old people lining up for soup rations from UN trucks, and parents burying their dead children. We see families escaping in terror from their towns and villages and bearing witness to the slaughter of their neighbors. And we somehow imagine that they can handle this better than we ever could. Now we've watched it in New York City and Washington and in a pastoral field in Pennsylvania. Now we know those presumptions are terribly wrong. People in places like Sarajevo also watched CNN. They could hardly believe that war had come to their backyards in the 1990s. During the conflict in the Balkans, otherwise reasonable people said foolish things like, "They've been at this for centuries. Let them kill each other." During the crisis in Afghanistan, the same people said, "They never went to school anyway and women were always treated like this."

Not the women I met. Not in Bosnia and not in Afghanistan. The war in the Balkan region had already provided plenty of evidence that rape was regarded by the combatants as another tool of war. Eva Penavic, who was gang-raped during the war in the Balkans, was a grandmother of five, a leader in her village. She was passionately in love with her husband, Bartol, when the same men who raped her beat him to death. When we sat together through a long dark night in March 1993, listening to the nearby shelling at the front line, she insisted I try the spicy sausage she'd made for her family, and she poured cup after cup of strong Turkish coffee. She's not a nameless faceless "other." She's a victim not only of gang rape but also of an international system that saw the crime committed against her as one of the inevitable consequences of war. It was not until the year 2000 that rape was made a war crime, after an estimated 20,000 women were reported as wartime rape victims to the tribunal in The Hague.

The women of Afghanistan had been similarly dismissed while the Taliban tormented them, destroyed their health and kept them confined for five years. Sharifa Reza Mohseny and Frozan Mahram were teachers before the Taliban closed the schools in Kandahar. They liked going to movies and having friends visit. They went to the bazaar to shop and worried about paying the bills, just as most people do. Then they were stripped of their status as human beings. They have faces and names and laments so great they're hard to even measure. But they too offer food—sweet green tea and naan bread—to welcome a stranger to what feels like a prison.

Meeting people on their own turf makes us realize we aren't different. Their babies also get croup. Their kids also forget to do their homework. Their teenagers also drive them crazy at times. They had jobs to go to and rent to pay. They had their friends over to dinner on a Saturday night and took trips to the park with their children. But somehow we turn them into "others." Perhaps it's our way of separating ourselves from something we feel powerless to stop. But we aren't powerless. As philosopher Hannah Arendt said in her book *The Anatomy of Evil*, "Evil thrives on apathy and cannot exist without it." If we turn our backs on evil, our passivity translates into approval. Silence is consent.

I thought a lot about Arendt's words one night, less than a month after September 11, when I received a call from Adeena Niazi, the president of the Afghan Women's Organization. She was in Toronto, but her voice was barely recognizable. "They're going to bomb us," she said with a mixture of disbelief and terror. "You have to help us." She hoped that the women who'd been speaking out for the women of

Afghanistan would implore the power-brokers not to wreck what was left of their lives with a bombing campaign. But what could any of us do? The talk-radio hosts had already begun the diatribes. "Bomb them back to the Stone Age," said one. "Annihilate them," said another. I wondered why these same broadcasters hadn't thought about all those women and children who'd been struggling through a hell-on-earth under the Taliban? Did they really think that the women—like the ones I knew: Frozan and Sharifa, Hamida and Wahida—deserved to be bombed back to the Stone Age?

Surely in our high-tech war rooms a way could be found to make surgical strikes that would disable the Taliban, stop bin Laden and protect the people who had already suffered for more than two decades. A few days later an e-mail message circulated from an Afghan-American, Tamin Ansary, who responded to the rhetoric about bombing Afghanistan back to the Stone Age. "It's been done," he said. "The Soviets took care of that. Level their houses? Done. Turn their schools into piles of rubble? Done. Eradicate their hospitals? Done. Destroy their infrastructure? Cut them off from medicine and health care? Too late, someone already did all that." As for why Afghans didn't fight back, he said, "The answer is they're starved, exhausted, hurt, incapacitated and suffering." Moreover, it's tough to argue with a Kalashnikov aimed at your head.

One woman in Kabul had told the Associated Press, "I pray to God that as soon as America attacks, the first cruise missile hits my house and kills me and my family." I knew how desperate the women were. I knew how helpless they felt in protecting their children from the ravages of war. On October 7 the missiles began to fall on Afghanistan. When I watched the bombing of Kabul, I worried, as any reasonable person would, about explosives missing their targets and straying into residential neighborhoods. But to my own dismay, I found there was an ugly part of me that said, "Go get those monsters." However, when I heard of the bombing of Kandahar, my reaction was very different. I was almost frozen with fear. I kept picturing Frozan and Sharifa and the other women in the basement of the Institute of Orthopaedics, and I could hardly imagine what terror they were feeling. Author Barbara Kingsolver summed it up in the *Los Angeles Times* when she wrote, "Every war is both won and lost, and that loss is a pure high note of anguish, like a mother singing to an empty bed. No kind of bomb ever built will extinguish hatred."

What we don't see in the TV news footage of women who were gang-raped by the military in Bosnia, long lines of desperate people walking two-by-two in the aftermath of Rwanda, families huddled in camps on the desolate road out of Afghanistan is the silence. Like the Edward Munch painting called *The Scream,* they are witnesses to unspeakable horrors, and they are silent.

After September 11 everyone knew it was time to give voice to their screams, time to act for the "others." The voice that had stood out for me ever since 1997 was Dr. Sima Samar's. On September 13 I placed a call to her Shuhada Clinic in Quetta. She was sitting in the front row of history. The battle she'd been waging for the women and girls of Afghanistan for five years had become front-page news. From her vantage point in Quetta, the first sweet taste of victory was the sight of Taliban soldiers fleeing across the border to what they hoped would be a safe haven in Pakistan. She said that within forty-eight hours of the attack on New York and Washington, the black-turbaned Taliban who used to strut around refugee camps, bullying the thousands of displaced Afghans despite the fact they were in Pakistan territory, had nearly disappeared. "There's hardly a black turban to be found," she reported. Moreover, she said, "The Taliban from inside Afghanistan are crossing the border and shaving their long shaggy beards [the de rigueur symbol of Taliban loyalty] as soon as they are safely out of the country. Then they try to mix in with the people on this side of the border so they won't be recognized as Taliban. Even the mayor of Kandahar, Muwlawi din Mohammad, tried to make a run for the border. He was caught with a suitcase stuffed with American dollars and hustled back to Kandahar by a truckload of Taliban soldiers."

Dr. Samar had been silent for more than a year. The Taliban had made it clear that if she continued to speak against them, they would not only kill her, they would close her schools and hospitals.

But when the tables turned, Sima found her voice again and began to talk to the media. She reported that, almost every night, flights were landing at the private airports in Afghanistan that Osama bin Laden had built. Planes came from the Emirates with supplies for bin Laden, and they flew away with cargoes of opium. She said the airports were being guarded by Arab men belonging to bin Laden's Al-Qaeda, that no Afghan, not even the Taliban, were allowed near the airports. The noose around the Taliban was tightening.

Two weeks later the streets and even the health clinics in Quetta were deserted, as people sought safety inside their homes when George Bush threatened to unleash his own holy war against terrorists responsible for the catastrophe in the U.S.—and against the countries that harbor terrorists. But by early October the bazaars were full again and rife with talk of defections in the Taliban ranks, a new coalition government in Afghanistan and the presence of the CIA at the Quetta airport. Refugees arriving from Kandahar claimed that the Taliban would make bin Laden king after a victorious outcome to the war.

Despite the fact the borders were officially closed by mid-September, thousands of refugees from Kabul, Kandahar and beyond began arriving in Quetta. Some trekked over the mountains and through "holes" in the border. Others lined up in the dusty, hardscrabble desert town of Spin Baldak, a one-alley village lined with vendors' shacks that are filled with contraband and stolen goods. Everything from SUVs and chickens to satellite dishes and cigarettes greeted the fleeing Afghans, who hoped to bribe the notoriously corrupt border guards and get across the leaky line that separates Afghanistan and Pakistan. Once in Quetta, they disappeared into the well-established Afghan community to elude the Pakistan police, whose intent was to round them up and send them back to Afghanistan.

The stories the new arrivals told were mostly harrowing tales of getting their families out of what they feared would be an American bombing target zone—and their sons out of the clutches of the Taliban army. Even the students in the ultra-fundamentalist Talib schools were being snatched up by their parents and hustled into villages that were presumably off the Taliban's beaten path.

The mood in Quetta, where almost everyone claimed to have an inside line to the war room, swung back and forth between a sense of impending doom and imminent emancipation. One man at the bazaar who observed a shift in attitude toward the American intervention said, "When the Americans attacked Iraq, the streets of Quetta were full of citizens throwing rocks at the UN buildings and calling general strikes two days a week to protest. Today there is much less action." Homayoun Acheckzai, the director of Guardians in Quetta, lamented the lack of meaningful aid. "When we needed one Kalashnikov, they gave us hundreds," he said. "When we needed one bullet, they gave us thousands. When we needed one landmine, they gave us millions. Now we need a piece of bread and they give us nothing."

In November UNICEF Canada appointed me as their Special Representative to Afghanistan and asked me to return to the region to check up on what was happening to the women and children. The first ones I found were trying to cross the border between Spin Baldak and Chaman, on Afghanistan's southwest border with Pakistan. When the rickety truck they were in wheezed to a stop on the war-torn side of the border, Abdul and Feroza Qayyum, their two children, Ali, seven, and Sharifa, two, and three other children, orphans, with them, tumbled to the ground with all their worldly goods—a gunnysack of clothes and two filthy quilts tied up with twine—and staggered toward the hole in the border. A clipped razor-wire fence presented one last menacing obstacle on the road from Kandahar to the desert town of Chaman in northern Pakistan.

There they joined the wretched of the earth—almost four thousand hungry, cold, exhausted refugees who were trying to stay out of harm's way on a bitterly cold morning in late November. The Qayyum family, like the others, was on the run from the hated Taliban, the drought that destroyed their crops and the American bombs that threatened their safety. Once inside the Killi Faizo refugee camp, they were told to hurry away from the perimeter, as cross-border fighting was feared between the jittery Taliban on one side and the Pakistan army poised for action on the other. For six hours the Qayyums alternately stood and sat in the rock-strewn desert dust while proceeding through a registration process that seemed agonizingly slow.

Their daughter Sharifa wore a string of plastic pearls around her tiny neck and wanted to show me how her pretty beads twirled. But she couldn't keep up the game for long. The beguiling little girl was hungry, tired and cold. She was painfully skinny, and she was coughing and sneezing. She was also barefoot and wearing only a skimpy cotton dress on that brisk November day. She was pathetically vulnerable and at the same time sweetly hopeful. Her mother, wrapped in a burqa, tried to hush her. Her father tried to explain how hard it had been to keep his children safe. They both knew little

Sharifa was in danger of becoming one of the tiny casualties of the new century's first war.

While they waited to be registered, Feroza described the rural area in which she grew up, where there was no education for girls. She was adamant that her own daughter be schooled. When her husband suggested that she shouldn't have such a conversation with a stranger, she shot back from behind her black burqa, "You can't respect people unless you have an education." When I asked her if she would continue to wear her burqa, she heeded her husband's advice and said, "I won't talk about that right now."

The waiting for this family seemed long enough, but for others the wait was much worse. UNICEF's Jeremy Hartley, the emergency communications coordinator in Islamabad, had predicted that more than 100,000 children would die in the coming months if aid didn't get to them immediately. It wasn't as though these children were keeling over on the street or being rushed into hospital emergency departments by frantic parents. Instead, there were hundreds of new little graves, small mounds of earth covered with rocks and marked with colored pennants and bits of metallic string. The children didn't wail their way to death. They just quietly slipped away in their sleep or while sitting in the back of a truck, waiting for the kindness of strangers. "It's a very anonymous process, this business of children dying in war zones," said Hartley.

Like Sharifa, they had nothing left to fight with. They were malnourished, underweight and suffering from exposure. They had respiratory illnesses and diarrhea. In the refugee camps, they were sleeping on the cold desert ground. They died from preventable diseases, mostly because warlords had blocked the route for the help they needed. In the time it took me to walk the last stretch of the escape route the Qayyums had taken from the gun-toting commanders in Afghanistan to tent number 52-S in the Killi Faizo camp, two small children died.

When I asked the doctor what had happened to them, he shook his head in frustration and said, "They just died. I don't know why. The water isn't good in the camp. The children are weak. They just died."

For some children, death arrived in a more immediate form. They became, to use an ultra-sanitized term, "collateral damage" or, more accurately, innocent victims of bombing. There weren't a lot of bomb-blast patients among children because most kids simply couldn't survive their wounds. In November 2001, they were far from help, so if they survived the initial explosion, they usually couldn't get to a medical center soon enough. At one hospital in Quetta, amidst the chipped tile floors, the dizzying smell of anaesthetic and the Kalashnikov-toting guards at every corner, sixty-five people had been treated for bomb injuries, but only twenty-three had serious enough wounds to be admitted. Some of those patients were children like eleven-year-old Sath Muhammad. Sath was playing outside with his sister Permenia, seven, when they heard the planes flying over. They'd become accustomed to the sounds of the planes so high that they couldn't see them in their town of Khartoot in Rozgan Province, but noisy enough to announce their mission. "We ran to the house," said Sath. "Suddenly there was a loud explosion. I fell to the ground. Then I don't remember what happened." He was trying to be brave, lying in hospital bed number 11, with the stump of his amputated leg propped on a pillow. He said it was the other leg, the one with a ragged row of stitches from his calf to his groin, that hurt the most. In bed number 10 beside him, Permenia was hanging on to the hard plastic cellophane-wrapped doll the nurses gave her and didn't want to talk about her wounds. A patchwork of burns on her arms, legs and face will be life-long reminders of the day the fuel from a bomb that landed near her yard covered her with fire. Their father, Tajmusmmad, who worked as a used-clothing vendor before the war, said, "My children are not Osama. Why did this happen to them?"

Farther down the hall in bed 15, Saleema, ten, told me her story. "I heard the plane and ran to the house. I was almost there. The bomb didn't fall on my house. But the trembling made our boundary wall fall down and it landed on me." They tried to help her in Dashat, the village where she lives, on the outskirts of Kandahar. But Saleema needed more than bandages. Her leg was badly broken. They couldn't find transport and, furthermore, it was not safe to travel. By the time they got to Chaman, her leg was infected. Two more days passed before they could find a ride to Quetta. When she got to the hospital, it was too late. Her left leg had to be amputated below the knee. When I met her, the hospital staff was fighting to save the fractured upper leg.

Rehabilitation was only a pipe dream for these kids. Their families didn't have enough to eat. They couldn't find shelter. Fitting a prosthesis and teaching a child to walk again were a long way down the list of priorities. That was only one of the frustrating facts facing the relief workers. Others included the colossal amount of aid needed—one million winter jackets in size small, for example—the unstable conditions in the country that prevented aid workers from getting to the people who needed them, and the clock that was ticking relentlessly toward winter, a brutal season in Afghanistan.

Although supplies had been stocked up along the borders of Pakistan, Tajikistan and Iran, there was a shortage in the camps. At one I visited, recent arrivals hadn't had food for two days. At another, they'd run out of clothing. The kids were barefoot. The situation was desperate. And this was in the refugee camps, where the international community was able to work. Millions more were still in Afghanistan, hoping help would come. And ten times the numbers in the camps took refuge with families of the Afghan diaspora in places like Quetta and Peshawar in northern Pakistan.

Coping as illegal refugees takes on a whole new dimension for children who are often made responsible for the survival of their desperate families. In the back alleys of the refugee quarters in Quetta, an Oliver Twist scenario was unfolding as more destitute children arrived on the scene daily. Every third house had a carpet-making industry. Inside, dozens of children between the ages of five and fifteen were stacked up on narrow platforms in front of the looms. Their tiny flexible fingers make them the employees of choice. They work with lightning speed, hooking colored threads on the loom and pounding them into place. They follow complicated patterns hanging on charts from the ceiling and hop up and down from their perches to grab a new colored thread. When I met them, they all offered a shy smile and were quick to show me how to weave the threads onto the loom. But like other children I met closer to the front lines, they were all coughing. They had respiratory problems from inhaling the wool fibres they were working with. Their nails were broken and infected and their hands bore wounds from being caught in the looms. And for their troubles, they were paid the princely sum of 100 rupees (about 60 cents) when their team of little kids completed a 7x7-meter (25x25-foot) carpet—about a week's work. It was just enough to keep their families from starving.

The neighborhood was full of displaced Afghans, some of them living nearly twenty to a room that contained nothing but four walls, a plastic roof and a dirt floor. The recent arrivals told terrible stories of walking three and five days over the mountains, hiding from the warring factions, stopping only to let their children nap long enough to gather the strength to walk on. They were exhausted, sick, overwhelmed and wondering who was going to help them.

Human catastrophes have a way of confounding rescuers. The vanquished don't turn up in the numbers at the refugee camps that the UN has prepared to receive them, warlords take over patches of land between the needy and the needed, and garden-variety bandits spring up like cockroaches, crawling over convoys that dare to travel into the zone of conflict. So getting the aid to those who needed it was enormously frustrating to the international aid community. For example, UNICEF tried to reach the children in Afghanistan by sending in donkey convoys, a maneuver that became an epic in itself— 900 donkeys and 1,000 drivers shifted 4,500 loads in relays over 14,000-foot mountain passes. But it wasn't nearly enough. "It's difficult to move inside the country," said Hartley. "We've been pretty much restricted to Kabul, not because of a road block or a donkey's broken leg but because of the atmosphere of fear and confusion that's everywhere in Afghanistan." This was the dramatic photo-op stage of the rescue, but the big guns in the humanitarian-aid business knew if it was not attached to a long-term plan, the future of Afghanistan would be as bleak as its past.

Hartley's colleague Gordon Weiss reminded me that "distributing aid is not a matter of pushing it out of the back of an airplane. It has to be done in an orderly fashion. Just when we thought we had a way to do this, four journalists were killed on the road to Kabul. No one knows who killed them or why. You can't ask drivers of aid convoys to take these kinds of risks." But he admitted that something needed to be done to jump-start the delivery program. More than one hundred kids froze to death in a three-day period during the previous winter. By late November the snow had started to fall again. The mountain passes were going to be closed to traffic soon. The hard facts were that small, defenseless children would die because no one could get to them in time.

The aid community was facing an enormous challenge, with roving bandits, hijacked convoys and the sheer logistics of moving enough aid for millions of people in the short term. Said Weiss, "What's needed is stability and an infrastructure—

education systems, health systems. . . . The lack of those systems is what really kills people."

While you can't attribute the survival of a child to the delivery of a blanket or a bowl of porridge or a winter jacket, without them, the odds of staying alive, of warding off the opportunistic infections lurking around little tots like Sharifa aren't very good. Her mom, Feroza, said, "People in war get money and become king-makers. Omar won't lose. Bin Laden won't lose. If the rest of the world doesn't help us, we'll be the only ones to lose. I just want to live someplace where I can find bread for my kids and live in peace."

While the stories at the front line were desperate, when I returned to Sima Samar's Shuhada Clinic at the end of November, I found an extraordinarily upbeat community. "Everyone's planning to go home," Sima reported. There's a formula used by humanitarian-aid agencies that suggests for every day, week, month and year a person spends in a refugee camp, the likelihood of them going home decreases proportionately. After six years away from home, the likelihood of returning is reduced to almost zero.

What I heard in the refugee centre in Quetta flies in the face of those statistics. Everyone I spoke to, whether they'd been there for two hours or seventeen years, was planning to go back home. Sima was already fund-raising for the orphanage and women's shelter she wants to open in Jaghori. Hamida Omid was making plans to get her school restarted in Kabul. And the irrepressible Wahida Nader said, "I've already tied my things together, I'm just waiting for the truck." The women who sat with Wahida at the refugee school where they were teachers, laughed in agreement with Wahida, but they knew they'd have to wait until there was something to go home to—stability, electricity, running water. They were convinced that by spring 2002, they'd begin the happy journey home.

Hope isn't a word Afghans have had much use for in the past two decades. But the whispers of hope I heard throughout the sprawling diaspora and the wretched refugee camps strung along the border were heartfelt. "Maybe this time," they said, "just maybe the tide will turn and we can go home."

They hardly dared to imagine a coalition government that would truly represent all sides, a pouring forth of international aid so the country could get back on its feet, and an end to the misogynist treatment of women. The Taliban was about to collapse. Now was the time for change: for diplomats to cobble together a coalition government that would understand the contribution women could make to rebuilding the country, to establish a peaceful coexistence between tribes, and to repair the health of the sickest nation in the world today. The women in this devastated country have the skills, the experience and the moxie to get this country back on its feet. Without the women, how could anyone consider a new government legitimate? With them—and a lot of aid from the international community—the political landscape and the emotional wreckage of Afghanistan could be forever changed. The days to come could be the paradigm shift Afghanistan needs.

In the meantime, the deposed king, Zahir Shah, was bivouacked in his quarters in Rome with his Canadian-educated grandson. There they received delegations from the U.S., the UN and each of the mujahideen leaders who were still making a power play for a role in any new Afghanistan. The talk in the bazaar was that the eighty-three-year-old Zahir Shah could pull off a coalition with some of these leaders and the Northern Alliance. But they said it couldn't be done without peacekeepers.

Back at Sima's busy houseful of relatives, that was the conversation we pursued while Sima was making fresh cheese and yoghurt for dinner. She was also stirring several pots on the stove—rice that she sprinkled with spices, lamb that had been stewing most of the afternoon and spinach that she flattened into a paste. We talked about the new government. Would she be considered for the interim government? She said she didn't know. She had been to Rome to meet with the exiled king, and she was convinced that he wanted women in the government but wasn't so sure she could trust the people around him. If she was asked to be part of it, would she serve? She answered clearly, "Yes I would."

Her daughter, Tamanna, and I were dispatched to prepare the dinner spread for the family. We put a large plastic cloth on the floor, a huge plate of fresh-baked naan bread in the center and began carrying the trays and pots of traditional Afghan food that Sima has prepared. That was after a full day of surgery and patient care, not to mention quarreling with UNHCR (the United Nations High Commission for Refugees) about why they won't buy the quilts her women have made. "They're buying quilts at the market from merchants. My quilts are better quality and are made by the very people UNHCR is supposed to be helping."

We sat cross-legged around the cloth on the carpeted floor and indulged in the results of the culinary talents of the woman everyone in the refugee center was talking about. Her husband, Rauf, was there as well—nursing a bone spur in his heel, a problem his doctor-wife couldn't fix, which meant he'd go to Karachi the next day to see a specialist. Her mother, Khurshid, who is now seventy-three, sat with us as well, breaking her fast after she finished her prayers for Ramadan. Dinnertime at Sima Samar's house was like taking part in a conference on international affairs. The talk was about the losing Taliban side, the new government, the patients at today's clinic, the convoy they were sending into Jaghori despite the fact that other international aid organizations weren't moving for fear of bombing and bandits. It was a free-wheeling discussion that included the history of Afghanistan and the failure of the international community to play the right card when the communist government was defeated. And like most family supper hours, it also included a discussion about Tammana's homework. Ten-year-old Tammana was preparing for a test the next day in Islamic studies. While the supper spread was cleared away and Khurshid poured the tea, Sima helped Tammana to recite the verses of the Koran, but her heart wasn't in it. The phone was ringing. The air was charged. Eventually Sima's sister-in-law Maryam Yaqubi took over the task and Sima and I walked outside.

It was almost exactly seventeen years ago that she came to Quetta. Now she longed to go home to Jaghori. She said on that crisp November night, "I have a house beside my hospital there. I won't need this hospital in Quetta because almost everyone will go back home. I feel so hopeful."

In the meantime, conferences to shape the new Afghanistan had been scheduled in Bonn, Brussels and Islamabad. Sima had been asked to attend all three. In Bonn they were to discuss an interim government for Afghanistan. In Brussels, fifty Afghan women leaders were scheduled to meet with world leaders and activists such as the European Women's Lobby, Equality Now, V-Day, the Center for Strategic Initiatives of Women, RAWA and the Feminist Majority. These organizations arranged the meeting to bring the voices of Afghan women to the political discourse around a new government, ensuring their message was heard. In Islamabad, the humanitarian-aid agencies were scheduled to meet, to prepare the next steps in the reconstruction of Afghanistan. Sima couldn't attend the Bonn summit or the Brussels meeting, but she did manage to get to the conference in Islamabad just before leaving for Canada, where she was to receive the John Humphrey Freedom Award from the International Centre for Rights and Democracy in Montreal. I asked her if she was concerned about missing those other critical meetings and again her reply was vintage Samar. "No. My voice will be represented at those meetings and it's better that I go to Canada and get the message about the needs of women and girls to another country." She knew that women such as Sima Wali, who'd worked for two decades at Refugee Women in Development in Washington, would be at both the Bonn summit and the Brussels meeting. Eleanor Smeal from the Feminist Majority would be at the Brussels meeting, as would Adeena Niazi, president of the Afghan Women's Organization in Canada. For Sima Samar, the critical issue was getting the information out, so that citizens around the world could pressure the power-brokers to consider the women when they sat down to carve out a plan for Afghanistan. For the Brussels Declaration of Solidarity, see page 202.

There was a lot that needed to be said. Just weeks earlier, on November 1, Sir Kieran Prendergast, under-secretary-general for political affairs at the United Nations, had made a statement that underscored the need for women to speak up. "Women cannot be included in peace negotiations in Afghanistan because the situation is too complex," he said. Women around the world were stunned. His remark was in direct contradiction of Resolution 1325 on Women and Peace and Security that had been adopted the year before. This document had reaffirmed the importance of equal participation and full involvement of women in all efforts for the maintenance and promotion of peace and security, and the need to increase their role in decision-making with regard to conflict prevention and resolution. Prendergast's remark had been a grave distortion of fact. The women knew that without their input at the peace table, women's needs and human rights would never be addressed.

Protests had poured into the United Nations offices. And women's groups doubled their efforts to make sure the women of Afghanistan were represented at every meeting and scheduled on every agenda. United Nation's Special Representative for Afghanistan Lakdar Brahimi, a skilled negotiator who'd been assigned the difficult role of patching together a peace and reconstruction plan for Afghanistan, had set the stage when he met with a group of Afghan women on October 31.

Almost four weeks had passed. While we walked around the courtyard outside her home, Sima pondered the possibilities for the future while she plucked off flowers that had died on the vines of her garden. Dozens of large pots of geraniums were still blooming even though winter was nigh. Orange and lemon trees were still producing fruit. "It's late for them to be in bloom but winter is late this year," she said. Just beyond the fruit trees were beautiful rosebushes standing four feet high. One branch rose above the others like a rogue offshoot, standing tall with a single pink bloom. It wasn't the pink of a dewy summer night. It was a strong deep pink, the color that comes with fall and the threat of frost and the coming winter. The petals rolled back and exposed the layers of the flower, each with its own distinct shape, unique, unavoidable, like Sima Samar herself.

We talked again about the complicated, difficult life she has lived, and I asked her about her relationship with her first husband, Abdul. Had she been in love with him? She was standing beside the rogue rose, fingering its beautiful blossom and said very quietly, "I don't know what love is. I was forced to marry. Abdul was really a nice man; I respected him a lot. But I married him so I could continue my education. He knew that." And Rauf, her second husband? "We get along very well. He is a kind man, clever too. He helps me a lot. We're very good friends." Then it was time to go back inside and check on Tammana's homework.

There were dozens of fax messages and e-mails from people around the world who were supporting the extraordinary work she was doing—and the phone continued to ring. It had been a long day, and if the messages that night were a harbinger, it was going to be an even longer tomorrow. Her son, Ali, was away at university, so his bedroom had become the guestroom. Before sleeping, I gazed at the young family smiling from the framed photo on the guestroom wall. The bearded handsome man is Abdul. His arms are closed protectively around fourteen-month-old Ali, a cute little boy with tousled black hair falling onto his forehead. Beside them sits Sima, with long hair, a long skirt and a multi-colored sweater on the knitting needles she is holding. For all the world, it is a photo of a happy, slightly hippie couple with the child they adore. The photo was taken just before Abdul was killed by the Soviets. I lay down on the guestroom bed and wrapped myself in the pink polka-dot quilt that Sima has had with her since she and Abdul received it as a wedding gift in 1975.

The next day we bid each other farewell and agreed to meet again in Canada the following week, when she would receive the John Humphrey Freedom Award from Rights and Democracy in Canada. When I watched her car exit the airport parking lot, I wondered if I'd ever see her in Quetta again, or if her next address would be in Afghanistan.

Chapter 10

TOMORROW

A hush fell over the packed hall in Ottawa's Chateau Laurier Hotel in December 2001, when Dr. Sima Samar walked to the podium. Cabinet ministers and high-ranking bureaucrats, as well as Aline Chrétien, the prime minister's wife, had filled the room to capacity. They'd cheered and clapped as soon as she had walked in. But now they fell silent. Sima Samar, the most celebrated women in Canada on that day, looked out to the women and men in the audience and said, "I don't know how to tell you how lucky you people are. I take all this warm hospitality on behalf of millions of Afghan women who are hungry, who are homeless, who are traumatized. They don't have any hope. In Afghanistan a woman doesn't count as a human being. We are property. We are things."

Then she begged them, especially the women, to help her in the task that lay in front of her. "It's a big task. I don't have any experience. I do need support to combat these problems. I cannot forget that I am facing warlords, the men who always have Kalashnikovs, that are ruling the country." Suddenly she turned away from the podium and started to walk off the stage. Sima was overwhelmed with emotion and on the verge of collapse from fatigue. In two weeks she'd given twenty speeches, over fifty interviews and attended seventeen meetings in nine different cities. She had crossed the country on a speaking tour arranged by Rights and Democracy, the Montreal-based organization that was giving her their John Humphrey Freedom Award. Everyone wanted a piece of her—the woman who'd fought for her cause and raised money to keep her schools and hospitals open—the Afghan community that turned out in droves in every city, the politicians who saw her as the epitome of a woman's struggle in the halls of power and, of course, the media who scrummed her every step of the way.

Sima Samar came to Canada on an economy-class fare and was booked into bed-and-breakfast lodgings. Then, on December 5, 2001, when the announcement was made that she would be one of five deputy prime ministers in Afghanistan's interim government, the outspoken doctor suddenly found herself a diplomat. She was hounded for interviews and photographed for the front page of every newspaper in the country and shown on television news reports. And she was suddenly surrounded by police—not the Department for the Propagation of Virtue and the Suppression of Vice, which had tried to muzzle her during the Taliban regime, but the Royal Canadian Mounted Police. She told me that when she returned to her hotel in Edmonton the day of the announcement, there were two chairs outside her bedroom door. "I wondered if it was a custom in Canada." In fact, it was the Royal Canadian Mounted Police who remained glued to her for the remainder of her voyage so that she could speak out safely, not a situation the daring Samar had ever experienced.

When she accepted the John Humphrey Award and its $25,000 prize in Montreal on December 10, she addressed another packed room of politicians and supporters. As she spoke of the starving children at home in Afghanistan, she began to weep. "I will continue my work," she said, "so that women's rights in Afghanistan will be counted as human rights, and that girls will no longer be punished for having a notebook and pen in their hands." She received a standing ovation.

In Victoria, British Columbia, she said, "Don't leave us alone. If the international community had not abandoned us in 1992 after funding and training the most radical extremists, the past decade of civil war may have been avoided. We need your help." In Toronto she said, "Religion and culture have often been used as a justification for the denial of rights to Afghan women. In reality, these restrictions have nothing to do with religion and culture and everything to do with control and power." In Ottawa she was officially recognized by the Canadian Parliament in the House of Commons, where she received a prolonged standing ovation from members of Parliament.

To the Afghan community that turned up at every event, she said, "Come home, we need you." To the *New York Times* reporter who asked her if her model of a liberated Afghanistan was a Western one, she said, "Why should everything be Westernized? Liberation is not just a Western idea, everyone wants it." And to anyone who wanted to know what liberation means to an Afghan women, she replied, "It's a woman who has access to education, the right to vote, to be elected, the right to work, to choose her spouse. These are the basic rights of all human beings. Afghan women need them as well." As for how she felt about being chosen as deputy prime minister, she simply said, "I must accept this role. Otherwise they'll say I was the one who was shouting louder than anyone else, and if I don't accept this position, they'll say Afghan women can't do anything."

She told another audience, "The work I do actually is not very special, but the conditions in Afghanistan are very special. It's not easy. It's been very difficult. They tried to put a lot of pressure on us [women] but we tried to find a way to continue the work we do."

It was a propitious time for a woman to be taking her place in the government of a country known for its human-rights abuses of women. The UN had signed Resolution 1325, claiming women must be at all peace-negotiating tables, and the World Bank had issued a groundbreaking report on the economic participation of women. Elizabeth King, lead economist in the bank's Development Research Group, had co-authored a December 6, 2001, report that stated, "Societies that discriminate on the basis of gender pay a significant price in greater poverty, slower economic growth, weaker governance, and a lower quality of life." The bank's chief economist, Nicholas Stern, said, "The evidence shows that education, health, productivity, credit and governance work better when women are involved." The report also stated that countries that promote women's rights and increase their access to resources and schooling enjoy lower poverty rates, faster economic growth and less corruption than countries that do not.

The stage was set for the minister of women's affairs to officiate over the liberation of eleven million women. But just a few hours before she left Canada, it became obvious that the obstacles Sima Samar was facing may be insurmountable. The United Nations was not supplying housing or security for the ministers of the interim government. There was no electricity in Kabul, and the telephone system was not functioning. Samar's cell phone wouldn't work there. Her life was still being threatened. On the Friday afternoon before Samar left to return home, Ariane Brunet of Rights and Democracy arranged the purchase of a satellite phone for Samar. That way, Samar could at least stay in touch with those who hoped she would succeed. A few weeks later, Brunet's action would prove to be more prescient than she could have ever predicted.

On December 15, Samar flew home. In Quetta, a crowd of 10,000 supporters mobbed her. She had just twenty-four hours to acknowledge their support, organize Shuhada so that it would operate without her, pack up her winter clothes, say goodbye to her family and find her way to Kabul. When she arrived in the capital city, she asked a journalist for Prime Minister Karzai's telephone number, called him and said, "Where are you?" He replied, "I'm lost too. Let's get started." The task in front of them was colossal.

The streets of Kabul were full of men with guns, and women were still afraid to remove their burqas. The city's infrastructure was destroyed, there were no bridges or roads in working order. Communications, banks, courts, power plants, hospitals and safe water supplies were damaged or non-existent.

Sima also discovered that she didn't have an office, a staff or a budget. Women lined up at the door of the house she was renting (for $800 a month) and crowded into the living room to talk to her about their hopes and dreams and troubles and fears. She says she spent the first week crying in frustration at the size of the task in front of her, and the total absence of the tools she needed to get started. Sima knew she had another battle on her hands. And she knew where to find the warriors she needed to enlist. She hooked up her satellite phone to her computer and, via e-mail, contacted the international women's network that had supported her in the past. Then she alerted the media.

Once again, women around the world rallied to her support. They pressured their governments to channel funds to the

Afghan women's ministry. In the meantime, the Tokyo Conference, which gathered all the countries willing to fund the rebuilding of Afghanistan, took place, and an agreement was made that all funds would be funneled through the United Nations. That decision created a dilemma for Samar. Hers was a new ministry. It represented more than half the people in Afghanistan. The other government members had buildings and staffs reporting back to work after a five-year hiatus—and were starting their work from a foundation that existed before. Not so for the women's ministry. Samar had to start from scratch. She needed extra funding and extra support. Experience had taught her that there was no guarantee the funding would find its way to the Ministry for Women's Affairs. The women redoubled their efforts to see that she got it.

There had already been encouraging signs of change in Afghanistan. One of the first was the sound of Jamila Mujahid, the well-known radio announcer who'd been banished from the airwaves by the Taliban. It was her voice that announced the liberation of Kabul over Radio Afghanistan on November 13. A jubilant Mujahid said, "I never thought a time would come when I would be reading the news again."

In December, the first women's magazine since 1992 (when the mujahideen took over) came out. Called *Seerat,* which means "attitude" in English, it urged women to reclaim their rights and to express themselves by writing about their experiences. Three young women started the magazine and charge 2,000 Afghanis (about ten cents) for it. While the Ministry of Information has the power to censor the publication, the women claim they never make changes to the articles. Their magazine is crudely produced on an old-fashioned printing press, and the first issue's cover featured a woman being pulled along by a rope. Their dream is for a full-color magazine that features light articles as well as the human-rights issues they are addressing today. By February, another publication for women, *Mirror*, was also on the newsstands.

Even in neighboring Pakistan, which has had a major influence on Afghanistan, change was afoot. Dr. Tahirul Qadri, chair of Awami Tehrik district, said, "Social and economic development in this country would not be possible without the active participation of women." He also said, "By keeping women backward and away from the mainstream, the per capita income and the resources in the country cannot be increased. Even in unfavorable circumstances, women have shown better results in the fields where they were allowed access." And in a nationwide broadcast on January 12, Pakistan President Pervez Musharraf blamed the religious leaders and their madrassa schools and mosques for inciting hatred. "They teach them terrorism and religious hatred instead of teaching friendship and brotherhood," he said. He called for a new curriculum and banned the teaching of extremism, effective immediately.

On January 10, 2002, Shoukriaq Haidar, president of Negar, a support group for Afghan women, and Nasrine Gross, an Afghan American women's-rights advocate, and a small delegation of women were invited to the presidential palace by the new Prime Minster, Hamid Karzai, for a reception in honor of U.S. Senator Joseph Biden. At that event, Karzai surprised the women by inviting them into a private meeting room and asking for a pen so that he could sign the Declaration of the Essential Rights of Afghan Women. The document was written in June 2000 by prominent Afghan women exiles and supported by thousands of men and women—as well as world-renowned women such as Gloria Steinem, Betty Friedan and Catherine Deneuve. The declaration states that the women of Afghanistan are entitled to equality between men and women, equal protection under the law, institutional education in all disciplines, freedom of movement, freedom of speech, political participation and the right to wear or not wear the burqa or scarf. It concludes: "Afghan women affirm and demand for themselves the inalienable rights that had been assured by previous constitutions of Afghanistan. This is essential for a durable, honorable and legitimate peace in a country whose women have been experiencing so much suffering." For the full text of the declaration, see page 199.

Karzai said it was part of the Afghan tradition to give equal rights to women and that it was also in keeping with the laws and spirit of Islam. He mentioned the 1964 Afghan Constitution, which clearly gives women rights. In signing the document, Karzai and the interim government had taken a step forward for more than half the citizens of Afghanistan. But it would take more than Prime Minister Karzai's signature to alter the status quo.

There's a theory called the Butterfly Effect. It's based on the principle that everything in life is connected. Everything no matter how small. A physicist allowed that the flapping of butterfly wings can change the weather hundreds of miles away. The message is that when a butterfly flaps its wings on one side of the world, eventually the effect is felt on the other side of the world. In a CNN chat room, Gloria Steinem said, "We each have a lot of power. Together, we make one hell of a butterfly." She was referring to the women of Afghanistan. "The focus on Afghanistan has made us realize that women need a foreign policy, that gender apartheid is as serious as racial apartheid, and that the shared characteristic of violent societies is a polarization of the gender roles. We need to speak up as much for women as we would for a racial or religious group that also includes men."

On February 8 I returned to the country to find out what was happening to women in Kabul, to check on Dr. Samar and to try to find Sharifa and Frozan and the other women I'd met in Kandahar just one year earlier. The street scene was the first sign of change. Crowds of men and women walked on the street. While the vast majority of women still wore burqas, change was clearly happening from the bottom up. Forced to wear wedge-heeled shoes during the Taliban era, and forbidden to wear white socks—or any other form of stocking that might attract attention—the women of Kabul were making a statement, feet-first. Platform shoes, high heels, patent-leather pumps were everywhere. And hosiery was patterned, colored and very much on display. Even the burqas were at a jaunty angle, displaying dresses. Hands, formerly hidden, were very much in evidence while women walked together, talking, gesturing, and even returning the thumbs-up sign to me when we passed on the street.

There was a palpable air of excitement in the city—and music, which had also been forbidden, was playing at every little kiosk on the street. Reconstruction was evident everywhere. Every little jalopy seemed to have a beam of wood or a plate of glass sticking out the window. Canadian Major Shandy Vida, who's on a three-year posting with the Third United Kingdom Division, with 4,700 troops assigned to the International Security Assistance Force (ISAF), has been in Kabul since December 31. He said the changes he'd seen in the seven weeks he'd been there had been both impressive and encouraging. "The level of prosperity, the number of people in the street, the amount of commerce has seen huge changes. At first it was odd to see a fruit stand, now there's nothing you can't get in Kabul." They've gone from having difficulty sourcing food to being able to buy everything from computers to vehicles. He attributes the change to security. Kabul still has a long way to go, but it's more peaceful than it's been in twenty-three years. The usual honeymoon period, an initial euphoria when the shooting stops after a war, seems to have been extended. "When expectations aren't fulfilled, jobs aren't created and the power supply isn't restored, the euphoria usually turns to more upheaval. But we haven't seen that yet. People are being incredibly patient so far," he said.

Women were working again and not wearing the burqa in the offices. Girls' schools had re-opened, although the official back-to-school day was March 23. The students were attending classes to try to catch up on what they had missed. And the girls were writing entrance exams to get back to university.

I found Sima Samar in the living room of her rented house. She was sitting on one of the threadbare couches, with holes in the cushions, in the room that has acted as her office for the first six weeks of her six-month term. There was a long list of appointments—diplomats, country representatives, delegates from women's organizations. She received the visitors from 7:30 in the morning until 9:00 in the evening. One of her brothers, Dr. Ahmad Ali, is acting as her chief of staff. He's an anaesthetist from her Shuhada Hospital in Quetta, but is here pouring green tea and serving almonds and candies to dignitaries who have come to help his sister. Her driver from Quetta is also here acting as her bodyguard. And the studious Mohammad Azeem Besharat is her appointments chief—when he's not immersed in Afghan literature and telling stories about poets such as Rabia Balkhai, the first woman poet in Afghanistan, who was murdered by her own brother in an honor-killing 1,600 years ago—because she fell in love with a slave.

Sima's lifestyle is anything but ministerial. Her office, at that point, was a filing system tucked under her bed. She both eats and sleeps in the one room of the house that has heat. There's a poem on the wall, written for her by Afghan poet Ahmad Morid. It says in part, "With one hand, you rock the cradle, with the other you move the world." She hasn't been paid a salary yet and is paying the house rent, the petrol bill and the phone charges out of her own pocket. "It's February 10 and nothing is done yet," said a very frustrated Samar soon after I arrived.

The visitors each have an agenda to help her. One promises 100,000 pounds sterling to use for vehicles. Another has funds for office furniture. Still another says he'll supply tents for the event she's been planing for International Women's Day on March 8. And another says she'll help with school uniforms. This exchange results in a vintage Samar scenario. The woman wants to know what they need for the uniforms. Samar, a seamstress herself, starts rattling off supply requirements: cutting tables, sewing machines, material, threads, sewers, shears. When the woman asks how many uniforms she has in mind, Samar doesn't even glance away from the sewing calculations she is making and says, "One million." Gulp! A million uniforms. "What do you expect?" asks Samar. "That's how many children have to go back to school. They won't go without a uniform, it's the way it is here. And if we don't make a million, we'll be picking some children over others to have an education. And that's how we got into this mess in the first place."

Samar didn't feel the same way about getting the schools repaired in time for the March 23 back-to-school date. "If they aren't ready, let the children sit under the trees. We'll repair the building as fast as we can, but the children have to start learning now." For every offer of help, there are forms to fill out and project proposals to write. She doesn't even have a secretary.

But there was also good news. The building she had chosen for the Ministry of Women's Affairs has at last been vacated. Now all she has to do is get the equipment she needs—there is no furniture in the building—and hire the staff she needs to start the programs she has planned. Her choice of office was brilliant. The grand old stucco building was built in 1949 as the women's center and stands as a powerful and emotional symbol of the emancipation of women in Afghanistan prior to the Taliban regime. The Zainab Cinema—named for the woman who started the center, Zainab, who was a relative of the reform King Amanullah—was gutted in a fire set by the Taliban in 1998. The cinema, which featured plays by and about women as well as movies open to the public, had been a source of income to keep the programs running at the women's center—cosmetology classes, cooking courses, literacy training, gardening classes and vocational training. There were nursery schools and a playground for the children and weaving projects for the women. Samar was determined to have the center re-opened by International Women's Day and to host the women of Afghanistan at an event that would mark their new beginnings. When an official from the government suggested she hold the event at the Intercontinental Hotel because Mary Robinson, High Commissioner of Human Rights for the United Nations, would be attending, she replied, "Why should I take the commissioner to a site that has nothing to do with Afghan women? This is where the heartbeat of the women is, this is where the event must be held."

Her plans for the ministry are focused on advancing the status of women and examining the underlying causes of their second-class status. She plans first to create a commission of women Afghan lawyers who would study the constitution, Shari'a law and the Bonn Agreement. "The women don't know what their rights are," she said. "I want this commission to analyze the current documents and fan out across the country telling every woman and every girl what those papers mean for them." She also wants the women lawyers to examine other ministries and have a contact person at each, so the issues of women are included in every meeting, at every post.

The second plan is the cornerstone of the work Samar has been doing for most of her adult life—education. She called for literacy training at every level, boys and girls as well as their mothers and fathers. She also called for short-term training of teachers and accountants, and she has asked the other ministries to make sure they hire the women and girls. And she wants massive technology training, auto mechanics, plumbers and electricians and all the other trades that have been sidelined since the Taliban. Samar says, "The Taliban members also need to go to school and be trained. Without education, there's no means of earning money and without that, we'll have trouble again."

Her last initial plan is the introduction of reproductive-health classes to families all across the country. At first, her colleagues on the interim government were aghast at the suggestion and accused her of "trying to impose Western ideas." She reminded them that Afghanistan has the highest maternity mortality rate in the world, saying, "I'm not talking about abortion. All I want is to educate the girls so they won't have babies when they're still children themselves, so they won't die in childbirth, so the children they have are healthier."

She's also vigilant about ensuring that women be given a chance to recover the ground they've lost. For example, she asked her cabinet colleagues to give the women five years' credit for work experience when they're hiring. She also begged them not to consider women only for secretarial posts. When she heard that, of the 7,500 students who wrote entrance exams to university, only 500 were girls, she asked the minister of higher education to show deference to the girls with a 20 percent mark increase. "Otherwise the women and girls will never catch up," she said.

When we drove over to the women's center for Sima's morning meeting, hundreds of women were waiting to see her. None of them were wearing burqas. They want jobs, they want help, they want to congratulate her and share their stories with her. To my amazement, one of them is Hamida Omid, the high-school principal who'd shared her story with me about the day the Taliban came to Kabul in 1996. She had returned to the city on January 20 and looked like a new woman. She was grinning from ear to ear and her eyes sparkled. "I'm very happy, I'm back," she said. "Before I died, I got to come home and now I'm alive again." She's here hoping to get a job working for Dr. Sima but says if that doesn't happen, she'll return to her high school and, she hopes, to the radio station where she worked on the young peoples' afternoon show. Like many others in Kabul, her house has been destroyed and she has no money to rebuild it, so she is staying at her mother's with her husband and four children. "Even though it's cold, even though everything is broken, even though we start at zero, we are happy to be back. This is where we want to be." She told me that Wahida Nader, the irrepressible supervisor of Save the Children in Kabul when the Taliban arrived, is also coming home to Kabul from Quetta. "Wahida will be here in time for the school opening and will work again as a teacher."

Many women told me that the back-to-school day is the day they will shed their burqas. There will be thousands of people in the street. The menacing mujahideen, who still threaten the women on the streets, will be outnumbered. And the women will put on a show of solidarity. Samar said it would depend on whether or not the security issue improved. "As long as there are guns on the street, the women won't feel safe."

There are other issues Samar worries about. One is the appointment of Chief Justice Shenwari, who said he didn't want to see women's faces and vowed that he would continue to implement Shari'a law. "Karzai and I will have to have a fight about that," she says. And the Loya Jirga, the traditional governing council, appointed to choose the transitional govern- ment that will take over from the interim government in late June and take two years to prepare the country for elections, only has three women on it. "I'd hoped for 25 percent," said Samar. "But I suppose three is better than none."

Later that night we were sitting on the floor in her bedroom when the phone rang. For me, it was like a flashback to Quetta in 1997, when I listened to her give an ultimatum to the UN caller who told her there wasn't any wheat for her projects. This time the caller wanted to help. Sima rattled off her list of priorities: schools for girls and women, health education, human-rights education, and then she told him, "We need to get started on these projects. We also need to build the roads and repair our cities. That will create jobs for the people. But first we need to build security. We need a national army and national police. We need to help the people to trust the administration. If the international community wants to solve the problem, they need to send troops. If they want Afghanistan to be stable and get rid of terrorism, they need to help us build security."

She never stops working the angles. We poured one more cup of tea before calling it a night, and she said, "I have only a short time to do this. I'm not interested in power. If the Loya Jirga elect me to be part of the transitional government, I'll stay because there is such a big job to be done. But I can do a lot of work for poor people through my NGO." In the meantime, Lakhdar Brahimi, UN special envoy to Afghanistan, appointed her chief of the newly established Human Rights Commission. So one way or the other—as Human Rights commissioner, as a member of the interim government or the transitional government—Sima Samar will be playing a role in the future of girls and women in Afghanistan.

The next morning, I bade her farewell and set out for Kandahar and the last stage of my journey. The scenery was comfortingly familiar to me now. The first time I saw the harsh rocky climes and parched desert sands of Afghanistan, they struck me as a colorless landscape. Now I saw bronze-stained patches in the slabs of rock and rippled geometric designs on the pyramid-shaped mountains, mixed with occasional patches of green in the sands, which changed color from beige to off-white and brown and pale yellow, with streaks of burnt red. The flat desert and mountain eruptions look as though they've been art-directed and brush-stroked for a travelogue. As for the cities, the rickshaws, which once looked to me like little ladybugs waiting to be squashed by noisy vehicles honking them out of the way, are a welcome sign of commerce. And the roadside stands—with their endless trays of fat, juicy tangerines and bowls of almonds—feel familiar and comforting.

When the car pulls into Kandahar, the shrieks and laughter of children at play fill the air, a sound I had never heard during the Taliban occupation, when children were forbidden to play, even with their own toys. We drive to the Institute of Orthopaedics and to my surprise, the first person to greet me is Zalmai Mojadidi, my Danny DeVito fixer, who'd accompanied me on my last harrowing journey to Kandahar almost exactly one year earlier. "Your girls are waiting for you," he said jubilantly. And suddenly there they were—Sharifa, Frozan, Sima, Torpeky, Zarghona and Rozia. The reunion was wonderful, exhilarating, and very emotional. Everyone talked at once, telling me where they'd been during the American bombing, how they felt when the Taliban were defeated. And each one in turn shared her hopes for tomorrow. "Now we have freedom," said Frozan Mahram. "Every girl can go to school. We can watch TV, walk in the street. If a woman wants to wear a burqa or not, she can. We can choose our own husbands and they don't have to have beards." They recounted the fear they felt when black-turbaned men roamed the streets and walked unannounced into their homes. Sima Shanawaz, who had been married just a month before we met in January 2001, put her new baby boy, Tariq, into my arms and said, "See what I did." The paint has been scrubbed off the windows in their therapy department. Their wedge shoes have been replaced with fashionable pumps, and they no longer need to use an intercom to talk to the men they now work with upstairs. Sharifa Reza Mohseny says her six children can now have an education. Her daughter Sima, fifteen, who hasn't been to school in five years, told me she wants to be a doctor and take care of the sick people in Kandahar. Sharifa's husband, Ghulam Hazrat, who was a teacher when the schools were closed by the Taliban, has a job now as a supervisor at the Ministry of Education.

Life is looking very different from the despairing ordeal they were living through when last we met. "The bazaar is full of video cassettes and music," said Sima. "People are singing and dancing. There are marriage ceremonies. We watch American films on television." The rapid-fire accounts of their lives today were told as though to annul the long years they lived in what seemed to be a prison. They told me they wanted to travel, to see foreign countries, to have peace and freedom. They want education, a modern lifestyle, streets and hospitals that function. They used to be afraid of everything, even the staff at this center, even each other at times.

During the American bombing campaign, they were caught between fear and gratitude. Rozia said, "The bombing hurt my ears. We were awake every night, scared and hiding, and you couldn't hear anything for an hour afterwards." Zarghona said she moved inside the city where it wasn't as bad as on the outskirts. "I was certain they'd never drop a bomb on my house." Sima took refuge in the city of Ghor, and Frozan endured the bombing for a while and then left for Helmand. Sharifa and her six children finally went to Quetta. All of them were back by the end of December and early January 2002, and they all agree that they're pleased that the Americans came. "But the issue is, when will they leave?" said Sima. "We'd like them here, taking care of Afghanistan for four years, not forever." Frozan quipped back, "They're better than Al-Qaeda."

They described the red, black and green flag that's waving from almost every car window. "Our flag used to be white, a clean color. But the government was dirty, so we don't want that flag anymore. The new one has three colors. Red for blood and the martyrs in this war, black for the dark days we've lived through, and green for the fresh start in Afghanistan."

But some things haven't changed. They told me they're still poor, they haven't seen any of the UN money everyone is talking about, and Al-Qaeda members still roam the streets and scowl at the women when they walk by. We had tea and talked about families and promised to stay in touch. They posed for a photo with me and said, "This time you can use our family names and our faces. We're safe now. We're not afraid anymore."

I hope so. As my car drove out of Kandahar and started the long trek back to Pakistan, I considered their future and hoped the horrors of the past were finally over. My journey ended where it began, at the airport in Quetta, when I checked in for the flight to Karachi that connected to Toronto. Sima Samar wasn't there this time. The refugees in Quetta were packing up to go home to Afghanistan. It was almost exactly five years since my odyssey began. As the plane took off and circled over the dusty city, I thought about all the women I'd met—the mothers and daughters of Afghanistan. But mostly I thought about Sima Samar. She's the one who fought her own jihad, without a Kalashnikov, for the women and girls of Afghanistan. I wondered if her extraordinary effort to change a society and make a future for its women and girls would be effective. It could be. If it is, eleven million women will thank her.

Inshallah, Dr. Sima.

EPILOGUE

The rolls of razor wire lashed to the top of the ten-foot wall that surrounds Dr. Sima Samar's house in Kabul are a troubling sign of post-Taliban times. Recent events that shook even the tough talking Samar are an alarming reminder that a year after making headlines as the most oppressed people on the planet, the women and girls of Afghanistan are once again the target of an insidious campaign to annul their hard-won rights and silence their demands for emancipation.

During the Loya Jirga in June 2002, when the Grand Council selected a two-year transitional government to prepare the country for elections, the fundamentalists played another menacing card in the poker game of power. The leading Islamic party, Jamiat-e-Islami, proclaimed that Dr. Samar was the Salman Rushdie of Afghanistan and called for her execution. They claimed that she had spoken against Islam by criticizing Shari'a law in an Iranian newspaper in Canada. In fact, she'd criticized the Taliban's interpretation of Shari'a law, a reproof widely agreed on by Islamic scholars. The chief justice, who is also a fundamentalist, waited for the chips to fall before deciding whether to send the case to trial.

Everyone knew the real issue was the progress Dr. Samar was making for women and girls. When she was elected vice-chair of the Loya Jirga by the 1,500 delegates from all over Afghanistan, the fundamentalists made it clear that they would not cooperate with the government if it didn't back off on women rights. Then in a deal with the devil, Samar was dropped from the cabinet, the transitional government took office and Samar's case was stayed. Presently she is the commissioner of human rights for Afghanistan.

In many ways Sima Samar has become the canary in the mine that is Afghanistan. What happens to her will reflect the future of women and girls. And what happens to them will affect the entire region, maybe even the world. There's a giant global chess game going on in Afghanistan today. The stakes for control are high. Fundamentalists in countries such as Iran, Saudi Arabia and Pakistan are playing for the status quo: the control of women, the segregation of the country into pieces of turf ruled by war lords and the destabilization of the central government. Playing for the other side is the international community that made a de facto promise to the Afghan people: let us invade your country to get rid of the terrorists and your lives will be better.

Their lives are only marginally better today. By late fall 2002, the promised international funds had not arrived in sufficient quantity to get the country back on its feet. And although the government begged for peacekeepers, countries around the world had still refused to send them. Donor countries claim they cannot act while the government is not stable. The government says it cannot stabilize without international funds. The resulting stalemate is making Afghanistan a vitally important testing ground.

I went back to the country in October 2002 to see for myself whether the promise made by the international community had been realized. I was encouraged by some of the change that had come to parts of Afghanistan. The schools were open again—but after a much-heralded back-to-school celebration, only about 30 percent of the children had schools to go to. Literacy courses for adult women were springing up across the country. A common expression among the women is "I used to be blind," meaning "I couldn't read, so I couldn't see what was going on." Women were out in public again without having to be accompanied by the Taliban mandated husband, brother or son, and as many as 40 percent of them in Kabul had stopped wearing burqas. The university in Kabul had reopened and was teeming with female students. There were several new women's magazines featuring everything from fashion to fundamentalism. And hairdressing salons were doing a tremendous business. There were fewer women begging on the street. Health clinics for women had reopened, although hospitals were in terrible condition and doctors in short supply. Doctors in Kabul have been told husbands no longer have the power to make the decision about a woman's need for a Caesarean section. Rachel Wareham, project officer for Medica Mondiale, the German based non-government organization, says, "Men don't like the scar and tell the doctor not to perform a Caesarean section, even though the health and, in some cases, the lives of the woman and child are at risk."

The contagious enthusiasm to rebuild the country and reclaim the future for their daughters was still high among the women I met. But the honeymoon that followed the ceasefire was clearly coming to a close. Most of the women who had managed to find jobs were not being paid on time, if at all. And they were still afraid of the fundamentalist thugs on the street. Just days before the first anniversary of September 11, there was an unsuccessful attempt to ban the voices of women from radio and television. Girls' schools have been bombed. Acid was thrown in the face of a teacher in Kandahar as she left her classroom. There were reports that girls in villages were still being sold for food. In Herat, where four young women burned themselves to death to avoid arranged marriages during the summer of 2002, Governor Ismail Khan issued new regulations for women. He told them to lower their head scarves and make sure their hair didn't show, to stop wearing brightly colored dresses, to register with his office if they worked for foreign non-government organizations.

The governor wasn't the only force working against emancipation. The vice and virtue squad was reinstated on August 15, 2002. Under the Taliban, they were known as the office of the Propagation of Virtue and the Suppression of Vice (also known as the religious police). They're the ones who, for example, caught a young woman with a forbidden manicure and chopped off her fingertips as punishment. Now they're called the Ministry of Islamic Education and claim their goal is to end illiteracy—which means ending religious illiteracy. Some of their "students" who have failed the "virtue" test are in prison in Kabul.

There are girls as young as sixteen in prison for being caught with their boyfriends or for running away from home. Their cases are going to trial, but there's not much evidence that they've been arrested for legitimate offences or that the judge who hears their cases even knows what Shari'a law says and does not say about women.

The litmus test for the future of women and girls in Afghanistan comes down to a girl who lives on the Shamali

Plains in the ancient village of Mavi Hatu, just forty minutes
north of the bustling city of Kabul. Her name is Lima. She
thinks she's thirteen years old, but she isn't sure. She's never
been to school. Her mother, father and grandmother were killed
when the Taliban bombed the village two years ago. And now
she's raising her four younger siblings, who she thinks are four,
five, seven and nine years old. Her day begins at 5:00 A.M.,
when she rises to start a fire in the outdoor cooking pit. The
roof of what was once the kitchen has been destroyed. But this
girl has carefully stored kindling wood, cooking oil and kitchen
utensils in a broken brick alcove, and soon has a warming fire
ready to boil eggs and heat naan bread for the youngsters who
stumble down from their sleeping quarters upstairs.

The rest of the day is filled with cleaning the room where
they sleep together, hauling water from a stream to wash the
dishes and do the laundry, stretching the clothes to dry over
rocks and making the next meal. Lima's day ends at nine, when
she goes to sleep with her little family on thin cotton mats in
the remains of the house that was hit with rockets a dozen
times during the Taliban regime. When asked what she hopes
for, she says she doesn't know. Even if there was a school in the
village, Lima says there wouldn't be time for her to attend. She
has no dreams for her future, only the present day reality of a
life that is so tough it's unimaginable. When I asked her if she
has a favorite thing to do, she led me to the place she visits
every day when she can steal some time to be by herself. We
walked along the winding path to the edge of the village. I
had some cockeyed notion that Lima was taking me to a
playground or a field of flowers where she could act her age.
Instead, we arrived at the village cemetery. This is where this
blameless child finds refuge each day. She sits under a tree
talking to and praying for her mother, father and grandmother.

In another year she'll start wearing a burqa. When I asked
her if that was okay, she shrugged and replied, "I have to. It's

our culture." She tried on her aunt's burqa, and in a single swift move, she was blocked from the world. Lima represents about 85 percent of the girls and women in Afghanistan.

There's a long way to go. The transitional government has until June 2004 to prepare the country for democratic elections and to produce a constitution that is unambiguous on the subject of women's rights. If they get it right, girls like Lina will have the right to hope, and women like Sima Samar can realize the dreams they've had for Afghanistan. In the meantime, they wait, and the women rely on the only tools they've ever had— moral courage and the tenacious belief that they can, and must, change the lives of their daughters.

Sally Armstrong
January 2003

DECLARATION OF THE ESSENTIAL RIGHTS OF AFGHAN WOMEN

Dushanbe, Tajikistan, June 28, 2000

SECTION I

Considering that the Universal Declaration of Human Rights, as well as the international statements addressing the rights of women listed in Section II of this document, are systematically trampled in Afghanistan today.

Considering that all the rules imposed by the Taliban concerning women are in total opposition to the international conventions cited in Section II of this document.

205

Considering that torture and inhumane and degrading treatment imposed by the Taliban on women, as active members of society, have put Afghan society in danger.

Considering that the daily violence directed against the women of Afghanistan causes, for each one of them, a state of profound distress.

Considering that, under conditions devoid of their rights, women find themselves and their children in a situation of permanent danger.

Considering that discrimination on the basis of gender, race, religion, ethnicity and language is the source of insults, beatings, stoning and other forms of violence.

Considering that poverty and the lack of freedom of movement pushes women into prostitution, involuntary exile, forced marriages, and the selling and trafficking of their daughters.

Considering the severe and tragic conditions of more than twenty years of war in Afghanistan.

SECTION II

The Declaration which follows is derived from the following documents:

- United Nations Charter
- Universal Declaration of Human Rights
- International Covenant on Economic, Social and Cultural Rights
- International Covenant on Civil and Political Rights
- Convention on the Rights of the Child
- Convention on the Elimination of All Forms of Discrimination Against Women
- Declaration on the Elimination of Violence Against Women
- The Human Rights of Women
- The Beijing Declaration
- The Afghan Constitution of 1964
- The Afghan Constitution of 1977

SECTION III

The fundamental right of Afghan women, as for all human beings, is life with dignity, which includes the following rights:

1. The right to equality between men and women and the right to the elimination of all forms of discrimination and segregation, based on gender, race or religion.
2. The right to personal safety and to freedom from torture or inhumane or degrading treatment.
3. The right to physical and mental health for women and their children.
4. The right to equal protection under the law.
5. The right to institutional education in all the intellectual and physical disciplines.
6. The right to just and favorable conditions of work.
7. The right to move about freely and independently.
8. The right to freedom of thought, speech, assembly and political participation.
9. The right to wear or not to wear the chadari (burqa) or the scarf.
10. The right to participate in cultural activities including theatre, music and sports.

SECTION IV

This Declaration developed by Afghan women is a statement, affirmation and emphasis of those essential rights that we Afghan women own for ourselves and for all other Afghan women. It is a document that the State of Afghanistan must respect and implement.

This document, at this moment in time, is a draft that, in the course of time, will be amended and completed by Afghan women.

BRUSSELS DECLARATION OF SOLIDARITY

In solidarity with the Afghan women gathered in Brussels, December 4–5th [2001], women's rights activists from Belgium, Croatia, France, India, Italy, Jordan, Morocco, Netherlands, Pakistan, Palestine, Somalia, Tajikistan, Tunisia, Turkey, United Kingdom and the United States met in parallel session in Brussels to formulate support stategies for the implementation of the Brussels Proclamation issued by the Afghan Women's Summit. A number of initiatives were devised by this group, which included activists from war-torn countries, artists, lawyers, funders and a parliamentarian. Also working with the group were the gender advisor to the UN secretary-general and the executive director of

UNIFEM. The group was deeply moved and inspired by the clarity and brilliance of the Brussels Proclamation and the vision of Afghan women for the future of their country. In support of this vision, the group made the following commitments:

- To undertake an advocacy campaign to ensure that the funds allocated by the international community for the reconstruction of Afghanistan are conditional on (i) the participation by woman in decision-making over the granting of the funds; (ii) the inclusion of women's non-governmental organizations among recipients of the funds; and (iii) the use of the funds for implementation of the priorities outlined in the Brussels Proclamation.
- To declare on International Women's Day, 2002, that for women "Afghanistan is Everywhere," which means that we are joined in solidarity with the women of Afghanistan not only because we all identify with their suffering but also because we understand that the same conditions of violence, oppression, invisibility and other forms of inequality that plagued Afghanistan are universal. We will use March 8th to mobilize a worldwide demand for the implementation of the Brussels Proclamation issued by the Afghan Women's Summit.
- To create an international task force of women's rights lawyers with particular expertise in drafting legislation and constitutional law.
- To provide political support to the Ministry of Women created by the Bonn Agreement, and to undertake efforts to foster voter education and the participation by women in elections.
- To coordinate a funding effort to support grassroots community initiatives by and for women in Afghanistan and neighboring countries, which will make available at least $1 million over the next three years
- To promote United Nations recruitment of women for employment in the various agencies within the UN system operating in Afghanistan and neighboring countries.

AFGHANISTAN— A CHRONOLOGY

50,000 B.C.E. to 20,000 B.C.E.: Evidence of Stone Age technology and domestic plants and animals.

3000 B.C.E. to 2000 B.C.E.: Afghanistan was the crossroads between Mesopotamia and other civilizations. Bronze may have been invented in Afghanistan at this time.

2000 B.C.E. to 1500 B.C.E.: The City of Kabul is established. Evidence of an early nomadic Iron Age.

600 B.C.E.: Zoroaster religion is introduced to Bactria (Balkh).

522 B.C.E. to 486 B.C.E.: Darius the Great expands the Persian Empire to include Afghanistan.

329 B.C.E. to 326 B.C.E.: Alexander the Great invades and conquers Afghanistan but fails to subdue the people.

323 B.C.E.: Greeks rule Bactria (Northern Afghanistan).

50 C.E.: Graeco-Buddhist culture reaches its height.

220: Kushan Empire fragments into petty dynasties.

400: Huns invade, destroy Buddhist culture and leave the country in ruins.

550: Persians reassert control over all of what is present-day Afghanistan.

652: Arabs introduce Islam to Afghanistan.

962 to 1030: Afghanistan becomes the center of Islamic power and civilization.

1125 to 1140: Ghorid leaders from central Afghanistan take over the country.

1219 to 1221: Genghis Khan invades Afghanistan.

1273: Marco Polo travels across northern Afghanistan.

1504 to 1519: Emperor Babur, founder of the Moghul Dynasty, takes control of Kabul.

1613 to 1689: National uprising against Moghul Dynasty.

1708: Mir Wais, forerunner of Afghan independence, liberates Kabul. His daughter Zainab Hotaki makes history for women by negotiating peace with Nadir Shah, who came from Persia to rule Afghanistan.

1722: Durrani dynasty begins.

1736 to 1747: Persian Nader Shah occupies southwest Afghanistan and is later assassinated when Afghans, under the leadership of Ahmad Abdali, establish modern Afghanistan.

1747 to 1773: Moghuls are defeated, so are Persians; the Durrani dynasty takes over.

1773 to 1826: Constant internal revolts.

1826: Dost Mohammad Khan establishes control.

1836: Dost Mohammad Khan is proclaimed Commander of the Faithful and is reunifying the whole of Afghanistan when the British invade Afghanistan.

1838 to 1842: First Anglo-Afghan War and The Great Game begin.

1843: Afghanistan becomes independent. Exiled King Mohammad Khan occupies the throne.

1865: Russia invades.

1873: Russia establishes a fixed boundary and promises to respect Afghanistan's territorial integrity.

1878: Second Anglo-Afghan war begins.

1880: Battle of Maiwand—in which a woman called Malalay carries Afghan flag after the soldiers are killed.

1880 to 1901: Abdu Rahman Khan rules and makes small changes in the rules for women. His wife Bobo Jan dresses without a veil and represents her husband in reconciliation disputes.

1893: The Durand Line fixes the border between Afghanistan and British India.

1895: The northern border with Russia is fixed again and guaranteed by Russia.

1907: Russia and Great Britain sign the Convention of St. Petersburg, which declares Afghanistan outside their spheres of influence.

1919: Amanullah Khan becomes king and begins reforms.

1921: The third Anglo-Afghan war begins. The British are quickly defeated. The first school for girls is opened.

1923: Amanullah Khan creates a constitution that guarantees personal freedom and equal rights of all Afghans, including women. His Queen Soraya speaks out publicly, calling on women to shed their veils. Women are given freedom of choice in marriage.

1928: The first group of Afghan women leave the country to attend school in Turkey.

1929: Amanullah Khan is overthrown, and Nadir Khan establishes control and cancels reforms.

1933: Nadir Khan is assassinated and his son Zahir Shah inherits the throne.

1934: The United States of America formally recognizes Afghanistan.

1938: Da Afghanistan Bank (State Bank) is incorporated.

1947: Britain withdraws from India, and Pakistan is carved out of Indian and Afghan lands.

1949: Afghanistan's parliament denounces the Durand Treaty and refuses to recognize the Durand Line.

1953: Prince Mohammad Daoud becomes prime minister.

1956: Close ties form between Afghanistan and the Soviet Union.

1959 to 1965: Purdah is made optional, women enroll in university and enter the workforce and the government. Women graduate from the medical school at Kabul University. Two women are appointed senators. Sports are allowed for women.

1965: Afghan Communist Party is formed secretly.

1973: While King Zahir Shah is vacationing in Europe, he is overthrown by Daoud and the Afghan Communist Party (PDPA). Daoud declares himself president and Afghanistan is made a republic.

1975 to 1977: Daoud presents a new constitution that confirms women's rights.

1978: Bloody communist coup—Daoud is killed, Nur Mohammad Taraki is named president, Babrak Karmal becomes prime minister.

1979: Taraki is killed; Hafizullah Amin becomes president, is executed and replaced by Karmal. The Soviet Union invades Afghanistan.

1980: Mohammad Najibullah is brought from the USSR to run the secret police.

1984: UN sends investigators to Afghanistan to examine human-rights violations.

1986: Najibullah replaces Karmal as president.

1989: Soviets are defeated and withdraw. Mujahiddeen make significant gains.

1992: Mujahideen liberate Afghanistan and form an Islamic State. Najibullah moves into UN compound for protection. Burhannudin Rabbani is elected president.

1994: The Taliban militia is born and advance rapidly against the Rabbani government. Mujahideen factions led by Rashid Dostum and Gulbuddin Hekmatyar reduce Kabul to ruins.

1996: Taliban force Rabbani out of Kabul, execute Najibullah and begin massive human-rights violations and the oppression of women. The Taliban control 95 percent of the country.

1998: Taliban capture Mazar-e-Sharif and massacre thousands of civilians, mostly Harazas. United States launches cruise missile attacks to destroy terrorist training camps run by Osama bin Laden.

1999: Exiled King Zahir Shah calls for a grand assembly to bring peace to the country. Northern Alliance, led by Ahmad Masood, welcomes the idea but ridicule the king.

2000: UN announces sanctions on the Taliban regime.

2001: Taliban torture and kill thousands of Hazara civilians. Buddhist statues are destroyed in March. Masood visits Europe to gather support against the Taliban. Terrorists suspected of being part of Osama bin Laden's Al-Qaeda attack the World Trade Center in New York, the Pentagon in Washington, and crash a plane in Pennsylvania.

September 9, 2001: Two attackers posing as journalists mortally wound Ahmad Shah Masood, the military leader of the Northern Alliance, Afghanistan's opposition to the ruling Taliban.

September 11, 2001: The twin towers of the World Trade Center and the Pentagon are attacked by terrorists. The "great game" begins anew in Afghanistan.

December 22, 2001: A thirty-member interim government begins a six-month mandate to prepare the country for a transitional government and, ultimately, elections. Two women are appointed as deputy ministers in the interim government. Dr. Suhaila Seddiqi is appointed minister of health, and Dr. Sima Samar, minister of women's affairs.

GLOSSARY

BURQA: a long garment, with only a grid through which to see, used by some Muslim women to drape their bodies.

CHADOR: a large (usually black) cloak and head covering.

CHADORI: popular name for the burqa.

HADD: Koranic punishments.

HADITH: the sayings of the Prophet.

HAJJ: the pilgrimage to Mecca.

HAZARA: one of Afghanistan's ethnic groups (and the most persecuted); descendants of the Moghuls.

HIJAB: loose clothing topped by a type of scarf worn around the head and under the chin; any woman's dress that follows Islamic principles.

216

IMAN: leader of community prayers.

INSHALLAH: God willing.

JIHAD: holy struggle or effort, not necessarily physical, to defend Islam.

LOYA JIRGA: traditional governing council.

MUJAHIDEEN: those who wage jihad; guerillas or opposition groups claiming to be warriors for Islam.

MULLAH: religious leader.

PASHTO: language spoken by the Pashtun people.

PASHTUN: the most populous ethic group, living primarily in the south.

PURDAH: a screen or curtain used to keep women separate from men or strangers; the Muslim (or Hindu) system of sex segregation, usually practiced by keeping women in seclusion.

SHARI'A: the code of laws or rules governing life and behavior of Muslims.

SHI'ITE MUSLIM: those who believe that Islamic leadership should stay with Muhammad's descendants.

SUFISM: Islamic mysticism.

SUNNA: the "path" or "way" of the Prophet.

SUNNAH: the traditions of the Prophet.

SUNNI MUSLIMS: those who recognize no divinely guided heir to the Prophet's spiritual authority.

SURAH: one of the chapters (sections) of the Koran.

WAHHABISM: a back-to-basics reform movement within Sunni Islam.

ZINA: un-Islamic sexual practices.

INDEX